Hand Luggage

Hand Luggage

A PERSONAL ANTHOLOGY

John Bayley

CONTINUUM
London and New York

Continuum

The Tower Building   370 Lexington Avenue
11 York Road   New York
London SE1 7NX   NY 10017-6503

Introduction and this arrangement © 2001 John Bayley

First published in Great Britain in 2001

For copyright in quoted material, see Acknowledgements.

ISBN 0-8264-5454-2 (hbk)
ISBN 0-8264-5774-6 (pbk)

Designed and typeset by Kenneth Burnley, Wirral, Cheshire.
Printed and bound in Great Britain.

Contents

Introduction

It is, possibly, a good thing to go through life with something useless for the mind to carry, a daily supply of that which not only remains memorable, but which can also act as a diversion from daily business and a consolation in daily anxiety. This should not be a matter of learning, or of the systematic conquest of knowledge: such heavy baggage is best left to the scholars and experts, those who make themselves the masters of a given field. What travels most easily and most engagingly in our daily consciousness can be lost and regained from day to day; it becomes a mental habit, an addiction which there is no need to worry about – and the words in which consciousness most takes its pleasure are also ones easily replaced if temporarily mislaid.

Something so mislaid may come back into one's head in the early morning, usually misremembered:

> Oh for my sake do you with fortune chide:
> The guilty goddess of my harmful deeds . . .

So long as the ear is true, it hardly matters if we misplace a word or supply a substitute. Instinct tells us that Shakespeare is not only a magician with words but also a tolerant and good-humoured one. He wouldn't frown possessively and be irritated if misquoted, and it is surprising how often even the knowledgeable get him slightly wrong. And yet he comes naturally into our consciousness; as young Crawford rather smugly observes in *Mansfield Park*, he lives in the English bloodstream. To quote him felicitously used to be the sign of an educated man, but we do better today by consorting with him only in the mind, carrying him in the consciousness as a mute but always friendly companion.

The things that come and go and are carried about with us in this way are not always verbal. It might be a picture that comes into the mind's eye: a sandy road winding uphill between poplars or among gorse bushes with a marshy pool at one side, blue in the sunlight. Have we seen it ourselves at some time? Or have we seen a picture of it? Which, it does not matter – the effect is the same. Or it may be more definitely a picture – say of a boat putting out to sea in the heat of a southern noon, a masked man at the tiller, a fisher king as passenger – his queen? We may even remember the name of the artist, or it may be just out of reach – never mind, it will come to us presently.

> The immortal goddess, with curving apple cheek, her bow uplifted, bounds with graceful ruthless indifference across the foreground, while further back, in an underworld of indifferent light, the doll-like figure of Actaeon falls swiftly to the onslaught of the dogs. A stream flashes, a distant mysterious horseman passes. The woods, the air are of a russet brown so intense and frightening as to persuade one that the tragedy is taking place in total silence.
>
> It was certainly dangerous to tangle with the goddesses.

We see Titian's picture; we enjoy the words of Iris Murdoch describing it in her novel *Henry and Cato*; perhaps enjoy them more, and with a greater sense of harmony between them, than is the case if Walter Pater's famous rhapsody on the 'Mona Lisa' were to appear in the mind's eye: for that description, superb as it is, is apt to displace our own image of Leonardo's portrait.

Most of what we carry so lightly and easily in the mind from day to day is quite pointless: and that is both its comfort and its charm. It is like incantation, but more casual; like dream gabble, but more nostalgic and more beautiful. It belongs to us, to ourselves only; and yet we know quite well that anyone can share it, that it has been through many, many minds before and will go through many again, so long as human consciousness lasts. Milton's 'thoughts that wander through eternity' are as homely and habitual as their more homely and humdrum cousins: the images and words that appear unbidden in the passive mind, and vanish again with – as it always seems – a promise of further hours of comfort in store.

They 'come like shadows, so depart' but while they are present they can engage our consciousness with remarkable vividness and vigour. Or they may just appeal as something that is inexplicably still in the memory when it should long ago have vanished into limbo. The other morning I found myself saying under my breath, or in my head, or however one 'says' such things:

> Vat yow goet en trek, Ferreira,
> Vat yow goet en trek

The mind accepted it, like an automatic traffic barrier briefly accepting a foreign coin instead of ejecting it with a sharp query: 'Hi! – not valid currency – where on earth do *you* come from?' I pondered the matter pleasurably for a while, doing something else. Then it came back to me. A novel of Buchan's – *Prester John* was it? – about a Black revolution in South Africa. Oddly prophetic I suppose, but I neither knew nor cared about that side of things when I read it, moderately spellbound, at the age of 8 or 9. This little snatch of song in Boer dialect was twice repeated, and as I continued to think about it I remembered that it must have meant something like 'Pack your bag and go Ferreira . . .' Never mind who Ferreira was – the words had an odd lilting and haunting resonance.

Useless information. Useless survival. But I was glad for a few moments that it *had* survived, and I was glad of its odd little haunting flavour. It would come back to me again some day, as surely as a bit of Shakespeare sonnet would come back. The sonnet was a spell or incantation too, but it also offered something to think about. For instance, I had never before noticed that those opening lines of the Bard addressed to some person, whether a person in real life or dramatically conjured up, constituted an excuse, an apology for the self and its actions, an apology all too familiar in our own time, and probably in all other times too, when people blame their parents, the state, the system – everybody but themselves – for whatever misfortune they have encountered, or bad things that they have done. Shakespeare knew all about that and he had an imaginary goddess, Fortune herself, to blame for whatever had gone wrong for him. Why hadn't she provided better for his life? – isn't that how that sonnet goes on? Whingeing about one's hard fate or one's bad luck was as common then as now, and thank goodness for that.

All these things that swim into the mind, like quiet idle fishes, accompanying us soundlessly for a day, a year, and in another sense for ever, divide themselves into a small select category of bits and quotations – images too – which we can summon from the vast deep by an effort of the memory or will; and the much larger, more mysterious anonymous crowd which slips into consciousness quite unbidden. How many times since he wrote the lines have Browning's readers ruefully reflected, when engaged in some love pursuit, on the wry truth of his exclamation: 'Never the time, the place, and the girl all together!'; perhaps they not only reflected on it but quoted it with some bitterness aloud: to cheer themselves up in solitude, or perhaps to impress the elusive girl herself? Kipling's Beetle in *Stalky and Co*, after an encounter with the cane wielded by a schoolmaster who is far from being a master of the art of corporal punishment, prides himself on the aptness with which he recollects a tag picked up from Shakespeare: 'Strange how desire doth oft outrun performance.'

But the mind at leisure relishes – indeed prefers – the pointlessness of those quotations from its own uncharted and unknown anthology. The things it hardly knows are there. They can sometimes come back with a shock if some substitute is unexpectedly encountered, which often happens when the New Revised Bible is read in church. Listening absently to a cathedral service relayed on Radio 3, I was aware of the reader of the first lesson, a man with a fine strong voice, recounting

Elijah's experience with God. I was suddenly fully conscious. Surely not? 'A faint murmuring sound?' Surely the Lord of Hosts could do better than that? And then other words spoke themselves in my head. 'And after the Fire a Still, Small Voice.' That was surely how it should be? I might be misremembering the Fire, but I was quite certain of the Still, Small Voice. It was unforgettable. Why had they turned it into 'a faint murmuring sound'? Was that closer to the Hebrew or something? Even if it were, the Jacobean translation must be infinitely more true, more suggestive? Above all, more powerful and more menacing? That faint, murmuring sound could never figure in anybody's unconscious anthology.

This random anthology of the mind may be given to mis-quotation, but it can usually tell if something sounds wrong, and then supply from some unknown inner source the proper words. It also seems instinctively fond of parody, even a kind of semi-burlesque. It could be argued that all good writing, con-sisting as it does of words that achieve an effect and strike an attitude different from that of any other words, are themselves more than halfway to parody and self-imitation. Our own unconscious powers of recollection, storing and comparing, attaching and loving, complete the process. 'Not a drum was heard, not a funeral note', or 'There's a breathless hush in the close tonight . . .' Memory strikes its own attitude when it brings lines like these back into the theatre of the head. When my wife Iris Murdoch was ill with Alzheimer's disease, she liked to go to bed fully clothed where she lay serenely, as if safe at last, smiling up at me as I bent over to kiss her goodnight. On one occasion I chanted to her:

> She lay like a warrior taking her rest
> With her martial cloak around her.

She seemed to recognize and respond to the familiar lines, and after that it became an evening ritual. If I forgot to utter them, in a suitably defunctive but 'heroic' accent, she looked worried and upset. As soon as I quoted them she wriggled about in her clothes like a child and began to smile and laugh. The magic and emotion of poetry and its words, recorded and transformed for an occasion, appeared to be getting through.

The impulse behind such items in the mind's anthological display is handed on from one generation to the next. When we were alone together my mother used sometimes to mutter histrionically to herself;

> And how can man die better than facing fearful odds
> For the ashes of his fathers and the temples of his gods?

She seemed to do it for her own pleasure rather than mine, and I for my part thought old Horatius and his doings pretty absurd. I longed for the Etruscans to win and for Lars Porsena to bring the Romans to utter discomfiture. It was that tiresome Horatius's fault, as Sextus Tarquinius all too justly observed:

> But for this stay, ere close of day,
> We should have sacked the town!

My mother knew the poem from her own childhood, and knew it more or less by heart, although there were plenty of gaps in her memory and she never bothered about getting it right. It had become part of her mental anthology, but it was never part of mine. I respected her sense of it nonetheless, and her pleasure; but already I had my own small hoard of words and incantations that meant the same to me as Horatius meant for her. Such pleasure in spells and quotes and rhymes and words is inevitably solipsistic.

There is an element of harmless snobbery in it too. I didn't think much of Macaulay at the age of 7, but I changed my mind a year later when I found that I adored Kipling, and his characters took a very different view. Una in *Puck of Pook's Hill*, who must have been of the same generation as my mother, declaims the Lay aloud when she is alone in the wood, waiting for Dan:

From lordly Volterrae, where scowls the far-famed hold
Piled by the hands of giants for god-like kings of old.

I told myself, and there may be something in it too, that the
poem was only really good at the beginning, when the Etruscans were gathering their forces together and looked like
winning. It gave me satisfaction a few years later when I discovered that my idol of that time, D. H. Lawrence, was
definitely an Etruscan fan and held a poor opinion of the
Romans.

At the age when my mother recited bits of Horatius to me
(but really to herself) I was becoming an ardent Kipling fan. I
was electrified by the fate of Punch in 'Baa Baa Black Sheep'
but what really got me were the fragments of a ballad that
Uncle Harry died reciting, his voice shooting up a shrill octave:

And then came on the lovely Rose
The Philomel her fireship closed,
And the littler Brisk was sore exposed
That day at Navarino.

'That day a Navarino Uncle Harry!' screams out Punch, 'wild
with excitement and fear of what he knew not what.' Uncle
Harry was a retired naval petty officer with, he tells Punch, a
chunk of wadding somewhere inside him from the guns of that
memorable day. Like Punch I wondered what 'wadding' was,
and I couldn't find out anything about the battle except that the
British and Russian fleets blew the poor old Turks out of the
water with hardly any casualties on their own side, Uncle
Harry being evidently one of them.

I never discovered (not that I have tried very hard) whether
Kipling himself composed the verses quoted or whether they
were the work of some, as it were, real poet nearer the time of
the battle which must have taken place in the early 1820s. As
electrifying to me at that age as 'Baa Baa Black Sheep' was
Kipling's story about the Indian North West Frontier called
'The Drums of the Fore and Aft'. Sentimental and brutal

(Hemingway admired it, as I was to discover some years later), it describes an English regiment's rout in panic by the Afghans. The regiment is saved only by its two drunken little drummer boys, and by the Scots and Gurkhas who come to its aid. The martyred drummer boys left me cold, but I was fascinated by the Gurkhas and their *kukris*, and particularly by the odd chant they roared out as they rushed down the hill upon their foes. It seemed somehow so unlikely and for that reason so authentic.

> He kissed her in the kitchen and he kissed her in the hall
>   Chillun Chillun, follow me.
> Lor lummy said tha cook, is he gwine to kiss us all?
> Glory glory glory Hallelujah!

A great many years later I discovered it was an Anglo-American ditty of the time, sung in rough company and using a more robust word than the 'kiss' Kipling had substituted. The tale lived in my consciousness for months, and the scrap of the song that Gurkhas liked to chant with their Gurkhali warcry was even more obstinate. It has surfaced in my mind occasionally ever since.

At that age, and for years afterwards, almost all my life took place in books. I was briefly rather fond of Rider Haggard, and the fabulous 'She who must be obeyed'. But in some way I always knew him to be inferior to Kipling – more obvious, less real – in spite of the way they had been lumped together in popular fame. Some critic of the *fin de siècle*, I was later to find, had coupled their names in an ironical epigram, a languid wish for a time when:

> The Rudyards cease from Kipling
> And the Haggards ride no more.

That time has never come for me, although I could not really get lost in *King Solomon's Mines* the last time I looked into it. In any case, at about the age of 11 my mind became Conradized instead of Kiplingized, and I moved about in a cloud of sardonic irony.

Conrad virtually coincided with Aldous Huxley, Katherine Mansfield, Virginia Woolf . . . 'She gave me eyes, she gave me ears' my old friend and teacher David Cecil used to say of Virginia Woolf, borrowing the phrase from Wordsworth's fervent tribute to Nature and her powers. David Cecil had read Virginia Woolf when young and had known her well. I loved all her novels for a while, and her first, *The Voyage Out*, above all – though for no better reason than because it was the first I discovered. She soon lost out to the more powerful charms of D. H. Lawrence, whom I loved equally as poet, lyric novelist and letter-writer, although his own beliefs and theories bored me stiff, and have continued to do so.

I was fortunate at school. There was no formal English teaching in those happier days, but there was lots of time to read – particularly at the beginning of the war, to which many masters had gone. Perversely, I never liked any book, prose or poetry, which was 'on the syllabus', or which those in authority recommended me to read. Later on, when I taught English at Oxford, I was reluctant to advise too much or to press recommendations on students. I preferred to say 'Try it and see.' But that approach had its drawbacks. Some pupils of the more private sort responded to it, but I was often disconcerted to find that a majority were discontented. They preferred pack tactics: finding out what's in vogue at the moment and going for it *en masse*. To be left all alone by themselves among the shelves of a library can cause in many students an acute case of agoraphobia.

Now more or less in retirement I have come to feel that 'English' should not have become an academic subject in the first place. It is one that is better as an enriching amusement – 'a worthwhile activity' as Iris's old headmistress used to say – for the middle-aged and the elderly. The young who really want education (and not so many of them do) should face more intellectual and more demanding pursuits. The intelligent young will want to read books anyway – novels and poems of their own choice – and make up their own minds about them.

But this is a digression, one no doubt suited to the opinion-ated old bore that most of us become with age. A purely literary autobiography is of more interest, at least to myself; and my distant past seems full of books which, as Cathy says of her dreams in *Wuthering Heights*, 'have gone and through me, like water through wine, and altered the colour of my mind'. The Brontë girls' experience in the lonely parsonage was no doubt much the same as mine. Could that be partly the reason why, strangely enough, their novels never had any great appeal for me? *Wuthering Heights*, they say, is marvellously planned, and I can quite believe it; but I only really respond to the ending, which seems to me more like the fragment of a perfect and very haunting ghost story. A little boy, minding sheep, is afraid to go near the Heights because he thinks he has seen Heathcliff there, with a woman. Lockwood, the narrator, is in the churchyard on a calm summer's evening and stands before their graves – Heathcliff's and Cathy's. He lingers there under the benign sky and wonders how anyone 'could imagine unquiet slumbers for the sleepers in that quiet earth'. It is the last sentence in the book and it is not ironical. Mr Lockwood may be a bit of a fool, but I have always felt inclined to agree with him: perhaps a lot of readers do. The book, like many other novels of gothic passions, has tried to persuade us to imagine, and at least temporarily to believe, such things, but admits in the end that they will hardly do. Perhaps Emily Brontë was ultimately too sensible a woman, too down to earth? She did not quite believe in her own fantasy? However that may be, her ending continues to give us in a few impassive paragraphs, the truth of why we can be persuaded to believe in the ghostly, and also why we don't really believe in it.

Although I felt I ought to like the Brontës (and I even read a paper on *Wuthering Heights* to the school Literary Society) the writer whom I became really at home with was Thomas Hardy. I liked his homelier side – I did not greatly respond to him as a writer of tragic power. I became a devotee of his more obscure novels like *A Laodicean* and *A Pair of Blue Eyes*, even his first to be published, the complex and unintentionally comic melo-drama, *Desperate Remedies*.

Feeling myself, affecting to feel myself, as a solitary figure, shunning social life and the conventional or fashionable books that went with it, I admired Hardy as an autodidactic who educated himself by solitary reading; certainly his earlier novels show a naïve pride in the possession of out-of-the-way know-ledge. I loved too the more natural way in which he set before the reader the interior life of cottages and the slow, humorous speech of country dwellers. My favourite character was Gabriel Oak in *Far From the Madding Crowd*, keeping his flock by night on the bare upland, and watching with a countryman's knowledge what Hardy in a later poem called 'the full-starred heavens that winter sees'. I hardly knew Hardy's poems at all at that time, apart from one or two out of anthologies. A passion for all his poems, down to the most minor and trivial ones, overwhelmed me much later on, almost in middle age; and later still I was struck by Philip Larkin's comment – he being a poet whom Hardy's verse had greatly influenced – that he wouldn't have been without a single one of the voluminous contents of Hardy's collections.

Other writers who strongly appealed at school were rather more suited to the time and place. I was attached to M. R. James' ghost stories, particularly to the settings and style of their openings, and I wrote several parodic imitations which have long since disappeared. I love Housman and *A Shropshire Lad*, and I also appreciated Hugh Kingsmill's little parodies of their spirit and content. 'What, still alive at twenty-two?' and 'Bacon's not the only thing that's cured by hanging in a string.' I also discovered Max Beerbohm's delightful parody of a Hardy poem, which comes later on in this anthology; and I greatly enjoy Beerbohm's series of tongue-in-cheek stories, *Seven Men*. His poem about Hardy's entertaining the Prince of Wales to lunch is remarkable for the gentle delicacy with which the parodist brings out the wholly peculiar and characteristic comedy of Hardy's vocabulary: 'To see you I'm unglad.' 'Unglad' is a coinage which Hardy would certainly have taken pleasure in using, had he happened to think of it.

The best parody, in fact, works in two different ways. It can exaggerate the special idiosyncrasies of the original so as to draw our attention, humorously yet also revealingly, to the way they work. But it can also achieve both a comic and a lyrical effect by doing something quite unexpected and far from the nature of the original. Gavin Ewart's extremely engaging and all too little known verses on the 'Larkin Car Wash' manage to do both things, as I hope the reader who finds them here will agree. The poem presents the spirit of Larkin in a bizarre and unusual form and also brings out the verbal and psychological background which builds up a Larkin poem. A charming example of the unexpected type of parody appeared in John Julius Norwich's 'Christmas Cracker' a few years back. Housman again was the favourite subject, but this is Housman in a most unusual mood:

> In Spring the hawthorn scatters
> Its snow along the hedge,
> And thoughts of country matters
> Run strong on Wenlock Edge . . .

> Her mouth was soft and willing,
> Her eyes were like the sea;
> I offered her a shilling
> If she would lie with me.

> At that she blushed so sweetly
> And cast her fine eyes down;
> Then, whispering discreetly,
> Suggested half a crown.

This Shropshire Lass was the delightful work of John Julius's friend Roy Dean, a famous master of parody and also of palindromes. As it happened I had suggested to John Julius a year or two earlier a superb parody of a villanelle by the Oxford don C. S. Lewis, included in this collection of unponderous pieces, which one can carry easily about in the mind. Who but Lewis

– not a particularly humorous man but an immensely curious and learned one – would have thought of wondering what happened to that ghostly Monsieur Cliquot 'Whose widow made the world so gay.' Lewis himself was a friendly and genial soul, but of blunt, not to say coarse manners, inherited from the trenches of 1917–18. When his colleague J. R. R. Tolkien was reading him an early draft of *The Lord of the Rings*, he groaned 'Oh, I say, Tolkien, not another fucking elf!' The robust adjective was then more uncommon in polite or academic circles than it has since become.

It is only when one is young that one is, so to speak, helpless before the power of books, poems and books that go through and through one like that wine through the water. The memory of youth holds what has no value without effort and even without desire. Why on earth should I have to travel through life with that little gender rhyme jingle in my head:

> And masculine is found to be
> Hadria, the Adriatic Sea

when marvellous verses by Horace and Catullus and Propertius which I laboriously learnt by heart for my own pleasure have long since vanished away and been forgotten? Auden's definition of poetry as, quite simply, 'memorable speech' is the best and most sensible summing-up there is. But what is memorable becomes so in the mind by some unconscious, certainly not deliberate process. Some wise old person once suggested to me when I was young that now was the time to learn by heart the best poetry, because one would always remember it. Not true, alas. I shall always remember the things that went unknowingly into my head at that time – fragments, lines, single words, bits and pieces; in particular, for some reason, a multitude of quotes of W. B. Yeats – but those long English poems that I tried to remember have vanished as definitively as the briefer and more pithy Latin ones.

But that happily dreaming helplessness before books and the words they contain – that is a memory that lasts, although the magic process itself no longer works with the books I read today. C. S. Lewis once remarked that we don't read books – books read us; and though I don't think this is as smart a comment as it is meant to be, there is certainly something in it. So far as I remember, Lewis – an old-fashioned academic and a combative religious apologist – was defending Milton against the critics like F. R. Leavis of Cambridge, who held that Milton's style was dead, his matter no longer relevant. Milton, in Lewis's view, was reading Leavis's mind and criticism, and not thinking much of them: in its own mysterious way 'Paradise Lost' can judge what sort of person we are. I myself was not particularly keen on Milton when young, but today I find I read 'Paradise Lost' with pleasure and even curiosity. Milton seems to have decided that I am at least worthy to read him in my declining years. But Virginia Woolf, D. H. Lawrence – so many others whom I once enjoyed so much and so thoughtlessly – would be a positive *labour* to read now, and if I pick them up for a minute or two I put them down with a sigh of relief.

All young people who have read a lot of novels and habitu-ally move about in the worlds that they create, feel an urge to write a novel of their own. I was no exception. During my four years in the army, from 1943 to 1947, I had virtually ceased reading. In theory I felt I could carry a book of poems in my pocket and read a few pages in the intervals of military business. But in practice I found it didn't work like that at all. Books and poems had faded: colour and meaning had been bleached out of them. There was something pathetic about the way they tried to stand up against what seemed the reality of actual expe-rience. I found somewhere a copy of Hemingway's *A Farewell to Arms*, and thought this must surely be something timely and vivid, appropriate to present circumstances. But no – after a page or two I lost touch and abandoned it, but later, after the war, I devoured it with a great deal of pleasure, even though it never entered my consciousness and my daydreams in the way that earlier books had done. I began to feel that, like Wordsworth in 'The Immortality Ode', the things that I had seen, or in this case the books I had read, I could now read no more. They no longer seemed able to penetrate the whole passive fibre of daily being.

But, as Wordsworth had done, I soon began to feel strengths in what remained behind. In Germany I struggled to learn some of the language, and found a new and wild excitement in being able to grasp and understand something of the wonderful rhythms and diction of *Faust* Part I: just as, many years later, I managed to break into Pushkin's poems, finding them and their language still more delicious and intoxicating. But this was more like conquest: not that divine insidious invasion of one's being by the books of childhood and youth. Yet in 1945 I determined to master young Goethe, and make his book give me all it had; and up to a point I succeeded.

It was much the same when I went to Oxford to read English at the end of 1947. I had intended to read history, for which I had obtained a scholarship at New College, but the temptation to do instead what I had always enjoyed doing so much was itself too much to resist. It was, in a sense, a miscalculation. I found that in 'doing' English I was no longer reading books, nor yet being read by them. I was studying them – a very different matter. I often felt discouraged, but there was nothing for it but to press on and try to obtain a good degree. I had already rather gloomily decided that the only way in which I should be able to keep body and soul together in the post-war world was by teaching. Teaching English of course.

After passing the Finals exam I was at a loose end. But books and reading, which in a curious sense I had not thought about for three years, while I had been 'studying' English, came once more – and unexpectedly – to the rescue. I fell in love with Sir Walter Scott, a writer whom I had hardly looked at before. Why the Wizard of the North, as he was known in his own day, should, at this point, have exerted a sudden fascination over me is a complete mystery. But I am inclined to think that there was a strong element of escapism present – as it used disapprovingly to be called. Scott's writing was so wholly unlike any situation or problem, actual or literary, that confronted me in my world: or indeed that of anyone else in this post-war period. I devoured him gluttonously, secretively, like chocolate – and there is a very great deal of him to be devoured. But what was I to do on the more serious line? I had a sudden brainwave: why not write my thesis on Scott himself? It seemed such a happy idea until I began to work, and then I speedily realized what a mistake it was. I at once lost all interest in Scott: I no longer wanted to read him, and I abandoned the thesis – in those more leisurely days no one in academic authority, at least in English, expected you to finish and present a thesis. In most cases they were embarked on for the sake of appearances only. I was still officially working on Scott; I had begun to do a little teaching. I determined to write a novel.

A sentence promptly came into my head. It was a question uttered by a girl, affectionate but peremptory. I started to write as if in a dream: automatically as it seemed, the words just tumbled out. In about two months the novel was finished. It was sent to a publisher who accepted it. That was amazing enough. When it came out it got good reviews, sold respectably, even went into a second edition. By that time I had given up trying to write another novel, after several attempts. Nothing happened. It just would not come, and it became clear to me that I was not a novelist. Something else made it clearer still. I was in love with a real novelist. A woman who was already a wonderful novelist, and who was getting better all the time. Iris Murdoch eventually consented to marry me, and I settled down happily to writing books of criticism, which was in any case more suited to what was now my profession as a university teacher.

I also began to find, to my great pleasure and relief, that I could write about the books I loved without losing them in the process. Perhaps the conversation of marriage had something to do with it. At any rate I really enjoyed composing a study of the created personality, and its relation to the author who had composed it, which I decided to call *The Characters of Love*. I was then madly in love with Henry James, and thought that *The Golden Bowl* was not only his finest novel but one of the really great novels of the world. Today I am quite sure it isn't, although I still think that in its maddeningly perverse way it remains a brilliant and fascinating performance. It's like life too: one can't be sure what the characters are really like, or what the author really feels about them. It seems clear that the moralist in him is at war with the aesthete, the man of art and style. This man admires Charlotte and her lover the prince; he feels them to be right, he *knows* them to be right, as a beautiful creature is right. And yet his American conscience knows them to be wrong. At the same time it is the woman who takes the blame. Stoical Charlotte is exiled with her ambiguously but beautifully civilized spouse to the wilds of America: the prince merely suffers the fate of a married man who has married for money. Money, for and by which they hoped to lead beautiful lives, is a callous master that makes the guilty couple its slave.

I pressed *The Golden Bowl* upon Iris, who was as much impressed by it as I was, and learnt from it too. But then she learnt from all sorts of writers, while as an artist being effortlessly her wholly original self, like Shakespeare. Above all she learnt from Dostoyevsky, who always remained a blind spot with me. I admired him greatly but could not feel at home with him in any way. I could not even find Dostoyevsky funny as Iris did, although the weird and matchless humour was the main quality which made me revel in Kafka and luxuriate in his deadpan stories. I did not find Iris's first novel, *Under the Net*, funny at all; but the unique and, as it were, absent-minded humour became that quality I most enjoyed in her later novels, particularly the one which is my current favourite, *Henry and Cato*.

When reading Dostoyevsky I keep wishing the characters would behave like ordinary human beings for a change. Iris's heroes and heroines are just as dedicated as his are to obsession or ideal, some principle of living and believing and suffering, but they remain fully human in the process. The furies or demons or angels that drive us, but which remain all but invisible in our ordinary lives and usually unguessed-at by the indifference of our fellows, are right out in the open in Iris's novels, as if the lid has been taken off the house of life and we are miraculously able to see others and ourselves in three or more dimensions. Power has become almost unbearably visible and is running about like a mad thing, pursuing and controlling, abetting and destroying. And the story insists on being read as if, among its many exhibitions of power, it has also been endowed with the power to force and to imprison our attention.

Oddly enough, it was while I was in thrall to Henry James – the later novels especially – that I began re-reading Tolstoy, browsing through him, relaxing in him. Wholly unlike James, he yet seemed oddly compatible with the richly untumultuous surfaces of the James world. James's words were as solid, as dense, as many-sided as Tolstoy's things. They were substitutes for things, almost things of a higher order, as Tolstoy's things themselves were, compared to what lies about us in ordinary living. Tolstoy, said a Russian critic, is 'the Seer of the Flesh'. He sees our bodies and their doings more intensely and more clearly than we can ourselves. And he sees things and people the same way, and, in a sense, with the same love.

So when I had finished for the moment with James and Shakespeare and Chaucer, the three writers I had been principally talking about in *The Characters of Love*, I found myself so absorbed with Tolstoy, and in particular with *War and Peace*, that I began to write a book about him too, which I called *Tolstoy and the Novel*. Tolstoy often asserted that *War and Peace* was not a novel at all 'as the form is understood in Europe and in England', but a form that had grown up naturally and spontaneously in Russia and occurred nowhere else. Maybe he was at least partly right, but he was nonetheless very heavily influenced by the battle scenes in Stendhal, as well as by the English novel. Goldsmith, Dickens and Sterne he uses with great cunning, as well as all the well-worn devices of the novel, while at the same time he seems to give us a simple chronicle of events in a nation's and a family's history.

The same is true of *Anna Karenina*, about which Tolstoy always firmly maintained that he had not made up a story or invented how it should end; things had just happened that way, as if inevitably. 'It is a bad thing', he remarked, 'when an author makes his characters do what does not come naturally to them.' He even claimed that he had tried to invent a different ending for the book, but that Anna always, always and obstinately, ended up at the railway station under the wheels of the train.

One thing led to another, and Pushkin was becoming as important to me as Tolstoy. My Russian was just good enough by now to let me enjoy him to the full: not so difficult, for Pushkin is one of the simplest as he is one of the very best of poets. He had just made the same claim as Tolstoy had done about his novel in verse, *Evgeny Onegin*. He pretended great surprise that his Tatiana had 'gone and got married'. This verse novel does seem to have a perfect natural symmetry, described by a Russian critic as 'the hero refusing the love of the heroine followed by the heroine refusing the love of the hero'. If that sounds artificial, the impression the poem gives – lyrical, comic, dishevelled, full of digressions, by turns lighthearted and deeply moving – is just the opposite.

I would like to have included a verse or two of Evgeny Onegin's as well as one or two of Pushkin's poems in this anthology, but, as I soon found when I was writing a book about him, it is all but impossible to convey by means of translation just how good his poetry is. In any case the obvious difficulty with any anthology, even one presenting a few examples or sample, to carry with one in the mind, is that too much tantalizing material pops up out of the fickle consciousness that memory inhabits, demanding attention.

John Julius Norwich had an excellent idea when he assembled towards Christmas the nuggets of all sorts that he had picked up during the year, sometimes suggestions discovered by friends, some of them from the rich bed of his own stream of consciousness. David Cecil's *Library Looking Glass*, Aldous Huxley's *Texts and Pretexts* and Maurice Baring's *Anything to Declare* were in their time admirable anthologies, as was Walter de la Mare's *Love*, and *Behold This Dreamer*. This last, my favourite when I was young, was strung on the loose guiding thread of dreams and visions, paranormal events and the vagaries of the subconscious. But, unlike *Christmas Cracker*, such anthologies are bound to have an air of the permanent exhibition about them, a faint breath from the fixed world of museums. What one carries about should be eminently losable and expendable from year to year: it will come back some time or other and can then be welcomed almost as a new friend. I should like to have put in this collection a poem I read and can't remember where – possibly in some anthology but more likely among the four or five green volumes of Georgian poetry I used to borrow intermittently from the library at school. It may have been an early *jeu d'esprit* by Hilaire Belloc; it may have been by some poet whose name has quite disappeared into the mists of time. I remember the first line:

'And were you pleased?' they asked of Helen in Hell . . .

It is her fellow ghosts in the underworld, ironically enquiring about her attitude to all the bloodshed and disaster she had caused. They recite a catalogue of the woes brought about by her escapade with Paris, while she listens, silent and smiling. Then, carried away by simple-minded excitement, she takes up the tale and adds to it. Aren't they forgetting the death of Achilles, the sacrifice of Cassandra and of Polyxena, the ten-year travail of Ulysses? The last line is the only other one I can remember:

And all for me! Pleased? I should say I was!

Almost the best pleasure of anthologies is to find things mislaid from the past, as well as some new thing whose stay in the mind may turn out to be as ephemeral as it is agreeable. Not only do these give the mind something to play with in its daily travels, but they can inspire its own flights of modest creation, sometimes to borrowing, which is a kind of harmless plagiarism. I once asked Iris whether the germ of some of her stories could be one of these playthings, which, in my mind at least were always lying about. She reflected, but thought not on the whole. Her mind, the mind of a trained philosopher, was highly organized: wherever those wonderful plots of hers came from, they were not suggested by the little nuggets of random association that casual reading leaves deposited in my mind.

Forty years after my first novel, *In Another Country*, I found myself starting on another one. Its origins were homely. Accompanied by two of our greatest friends, we were staying a day or two in Sorrento – a nice, rather old-fashioned place, like Folkestone I thought – and standing on a small balcony in the very early morning I saw a very tall woman in a purple bikini walk slowly down into the sea. A name popped instantly into my head – Alice! Perhaps because Alice in Wonderland grows very tall after eating a little cake labelled 'Eat me' and also finds herself accompanied by a mouse swimming in a pool of tears. At once I had a title and a beginning, and struggled along as best I could from that. At least, I not only finished but eventually found that it had grown into a trilogy, the second novel of which, *The Queer Captain*, was obviously inspired by the story of Rapunzel which I had much enjoyed as a child, and by Hardy's novel *Two on a Tower*.

I had written a small book on Hardy nearly twenty years before, at a time when I was simultaneously in love with his novels and with Barbara Pym's very different little master-pieces. It seems and is an unlikely combination, but my earlier passion for Hardy has revived in an acute form and got mixed up with an equal passion for Pym. I had quite liked the one or two novels of hers that I had previously read, but now I found myself a dreamy devotee, moving daily in a Pym world, and fondly reading little bits to Iris, who was – bless her – both patient and unappreciative.

Once, years before, when my old teacher and friend David Cecil suddenly asked me in his disconcerting way if I had read anything he might like lately, I rather diffidently mentioned a Pym – *Jane and Prudence* – which I had got out of the mobile library my mother helped with in the village at home. To my astonishment he became a Pym fan on the spot and for many years a more fervid one than I was. Philip Larkin, who had become a friend of ours, and my old pupil, A. N. Wilson, turned out to be fellow addicts, and there may well have been a touch of rivalry in this late love that suddenly blossomed between me and the Pym world. We were fellow worshippers rather than addicts, and I loved discussing her novels with Andrew Wilson, and more surprisingly with that admirable novelist Elizabeth Bowen – no worshipper but a cool and sensible critic who turned out to admire the unique and, above all, the humorous virtues of her fellow writer.

Iris did not read many modern novels, or know many novelists, although she was always very happy to meet them. She got on well with Olivia Manning and Elizabeth Taylor; Kingsley Amis too, who always behaved towards her with a great and slightly diffident courtesy, as did, in his own fashion, Philip Larkin himself. Both were chameleonic: they could be tremendous and rather cruel wags between themselves or in other relationships, but they both treated Iris with well-mannered deference, as if she were a highly distinguished maiden aunt: a fact that caused her some amusement. We were also very friendly with the tall and talented Candia Macwilliam and with another old pupil of mine, Alan Hollinghurst, who had done his thesis on the novelist L. P. Hartley, a great friend of David Cecil and a writer of subtlety and charm. The style and manner of Hollinghurst's own subtle and sweetly candid novels has a flavour that is not unlike Hartley's, brought entirely up to date.

Hartley himself looked almost comically unlike the rather Jamesian writer that he was. With walrus moustache and doggy eyes, he gazed at one with an air of comradely hopelessness, as if deploring the fact that he and oneself were the only two kindred spirits left in an entirely deplorable world. The other writer we used to know who to me looked quite unlike his own writing was Anthony Powell. Though geniality itself, Powell had a military air which sometimes I found a little intimidating, because it brought back memories of moments in the army when geniality and sharp censure on the part of a senior officer would sometimes and disconcertingly go together. The Bulgarians must have felt this when Powell attended a literary conference in Sofia, where one of his hosts, who knew England well, told Powell that he and his colleagues could not decide whether he most resembled a Major-General on the active list or a professor of Military Studies at Sandhurst.

I re-read *A Dance to the Music of Time* almost every year, as I often re-read and browse among the journals Powell wrote in his 80s. In them one soon becomes as absorbed in the events and routines of a small country hamlet as one does in the richly multitudinous panorama of the great twelve-volume novel.

One justification for anthologies is that the reader can get the particular flavour of an author's personality from a single poem or short extract, and then perhaps be moved to discover, or to rediscover, the work of the writer as a whole. And by the term 'flavour' I am not suggesting something merely metaphorical. Hazlitt has a most engaging essay on the associations by which we remember the 'taste' of an author, and the moment we discovered it for the first time. If he happened, years later on, to re-open Rousseau's *La Nouvelle Heloise* he at once recalled the taste of the coffee in a silver pot and the roll and butter he had eaten while reading the book for the first time at an inn outside Paris: so closely can mental and physical pleasures be allied with each other. A friend told me lately that certain odd combinations of flavour – curry powder and chipolata sausages for instance – infallibly reminded him of Iris's Booker prizewinning novel *The Sea, the Sea*.

That pleased me because I had had a hand myself in the preparation of the hero's meals in that novel. Iris asked me to write down for her some of the odd things that I had cooked and which we had eaten together, as consumed by her Charles Arrowby; on paper they sounded much odder and much worse than they did when we enjoyed them in our own kitchen. Never mind – they had sounded right in the book, and, what was better, memorable. The only other time I had made a small contribution to a novel of Iris's was in the early pages of *The Bell*; she had suggested (perhaps to amuse me) that I wrote a bit about

Dora Greenfield, to whom I had taken quite a fancy when Iris for once let me read a draft of the opening pages.

I think the instinct of all readers who enjoy novels is to add a bit more of their own, to leave their own print, as it were, on the page, and to feel in the book their own comradeship and participation. An anthology may help in this friendly process of liaison, as if we were being introduced successively to fellow guests we had never met before, or only half remembered. Taking up the threads of an old intercourse, or feeling our way towards a new one, is bound to be interesting.

I had a Hazlitt experience originally with Elizabeth Bowen's novel *The Death of the Heart*. I was in bed with some ear infection, painful but not serious, and my mother brought me tea and toast and a poached egg, together with the Elizabeth Bowen, which she had just borrowed for me from the library. Breakfast snugly in bed seemed the perfect time to read that wonderful cold beginning, to lean over the bridge with Anna and her friend St Quentin, and contemplate the ice on the lake, where swans 'in slow indignation swam'. The novel enchanted me at once and continued to do so. I know of no other novel in which the presence or absence of a physical *joie de vivre* in the characters is done with such ease and conviction, and such a natural feeling for comedy. The author's social sense is supreme, and has a kind of amiable ruthlessness in it which misses nothing, but never sits in judgement.

The beginnings and endings of great novels are often a study in themselves. Like the Delphic oracle, a good beginning can carry an ambiguous promise which lures us onward, not to destruction as the Delphic oracle so often did, but to a comparable surprise in the manner of fulfilment. At the opening of *The Return of the Native*, Hardy sets the scene on Egdon Heath as if for a stark drama or a tragedy in the grand manner, but in a typical Hardy way nothing quite like that actually happens. In Hardy's treatment the tragedy turns itself into a subtly different species – a wholly personal mode of fiction. Hardy is skilful at these transformations, and they do not in any way disturb the flow of fiction.

The English novel – and in a kind of harmony with it the

Russian too – has always been good at avoiding a single form and good at sliding unobtrusively from one fictional mode to another. We can see the process happening even in the case of that superb, not-quite-crime novel – Raymond Chandler's *The Big Sleep*. The plot holds our attention without requiring our understanding: which is just as well, because the author himself seems to have been unsure what happened. But, whatever it was, he makes the end of the story not only beautiful but strangely moving. The ex-bootlegger Rusty Regan had paid the price for refusing the favours of the degraded little Nausica who haunts the awful great house, with its English butler and Hollywood garden. His body lies in an abandoned oil sump: and the old father from a former and more chivalrous age who hired Marlow to find him will soon be sleeping the big sleep. (I remember reading – re-reading – *The Big Sleep* when I had failed to get some job I had put in for and was cheering myself up with whisky and dessert chocolate and Raymond Chandler, a trinity now in perpetual association.)

The advantage and justification for including such beginnings and endings in an anthology is also that they give a kind of ghostly microcosm of what the book contains in terms of its atmosphere and style; while a poem isolated by an anthology can sometimes challenge the reader's sense of its own mysterious life, and needle him into a new kind of concentration. Blake's intoxicatingly magical little poem, 'Truly, My Satan, Thou Art But a Dunce', begins as if the poet were rubbing his hands gleefully together. Then he drops them to his side and very quietly seems to shake his head over the piercing riddle of things. Is it God, or Satan, who rules the world? Neither, perhaps; for both are nothing but the hopes, illusions and consolations of a mankind struggling and dreaming its way through the dream of life. If we meet such a poem among its peers and companions in a collected volume of Blake, it can hardly confront us with the same force and feeling which it exerts on its own.

A work of art taken out of its own context can often surprise us in this way. It is only by disinterring a Victorian poem from its untouched, forgotten volume that we can reanimate it with the freshness it must have had when some young woman opened a bright new volume, and perhaps read a sample to a friend or fiancée. There was laughter, admiration, animation. Today the poem may merely seem dated, antediluvian, absurd. But by looking in a closer and more ultimate perspective we may cease to find it so.

Did such a Victorian couple laugh at 'Mabel I am waiting . . . ?' Rather, perhaps they laughed *with* it. They saw, or rather they understood without seeing, that the poet, Frederic Locker-Lampson – perhaps one of their cousins knew him? – was a humorous man, a poet of light verse and amusing pieces, mock-passionate but also touching and funny. Extracting him from his lost entombment, as Praed and Clough were once extracted, as Betjeman and even Larkin may one day have to be, the reader today can retrieve that unexpected and unlooked-for Victorian lightheartedness. The resurrected poems of Coventry Patmore and T. E. Brown tell us the same story. Their virtues can return them today to the life they must originally have possessed, and lost to the radical changes in taste and expectation which took place at the beginning of the new century.

Although I decided not to include any poems of Pushkin, I could not resist one by Anna Akhmatova, because it is not only a fine poem, with all her calm and moving dignity, but strikes a strange chord to match Housman's terse little poem on the same Bible subject. For Housman, the story of Lot must have been full of disturbing overtones, but he pares them down to a graphic statement of the divine will and its terrors, the burden of human sin that was and is to come. I should like to have included another favourite of mine from Akhmatova, 'The Grey Eyed King' but, like Pushkin himself, it becomes, or seems, or sounds, inadequate and banal in any translation.

The gaiety and magic in one poem of Pushkin at least can be indicated by a brief description, and this makes a suitable *envoi* for a traveller's book of belongings to accompany a voyage. Pushkin loved the season of late October in the Russian countryside, and in his poem 'Autumn' he celebrates its beauties, despising spring and summer and remarking how well his Russian 'organism' is suited to those first sharp exhilarating frosts and the promise of snow. It was then he worked, on his little estate at Boldino, scribbling away like mad and pausing only to ride out and enjoy the scenery and the weather.

The poem 'Autumn', written at such a time, ends with a graphic metaphor of creation and its inspired moment, the excitement and delight in the voyage that is beginning as a great ship, motionless on the still waters, feels at last the wind in its sails and cuts its way through the waves. The last stanza comes to an end and one triumphant line of what would have been the verse to follow concludes the poem:

It sails! Where then shall we sail? . . .

I hope the traveller with this book may share some of that exhilaration in setting forth.

JOHN BAYLEY
Lanzarote
Oxford
January 2001

Part I

DEPARTURE

Sydney Smith (1771–1845) to
Lady Georgiana Morpeth,
16 February 1820

There is far more poetry than prose in this little collection, for the obvious reason that poetry is so much more easily carried in the head. Sydney Smith was a famous benevolent and altogether 'human' parson of the late eighteenth century, and what he says about cheering oneself up is remembered almost as if it were a poem. W. H. Auden in fact makes a poem of it, which ends 'Take short views'. Certainly the soundest of advice, and in a sense the most easily remembered and followed.

Dear Lady Georgiana,

. . . Nobody has suffered more from low spirits than I have done – so I feel for you. 1st. Live as well as you dare. 2nd. Go into the shower-bath with a small quantity of water at a temperature low enough to give you a slight sensation of cold, 75° or 80°. 3rd. Amusing books. 4th. Short views of human life not further than dinner or tea. 5th. Be as busy as you can. 6th. See as much as you can of those friends who respect and like you. 7th. And of those acquaintances who amuse you. 8th. Make no secret of low spirits to your friends, but talk of them freely – they are always worse for dignified concealment. 9th. Attend to the effects tea and coffee produce upon you. 10th. Compare your lot with that of other people. 11th. Don't expect too much from human life – a sorry business at the best. 12th. Avoid poetry, dramatic representations (except comedy), music, serious novels, melancholy sentimental people, and everything likely to excite feeling or emotion not ending in active benevolence.

'The Cloud'

by Percy Bysshe Shelley

(1792–1822)

'Out of my caverns of rain' – a wonderful image for the way rain can look in really dusky weather, as if cave beyond cave were opening in the downpour. Shelley is brilliant at mixing the metaphorical with the factually and scientifically accurate, as he describes the skylark's song as disappearing into the morning sky in the same way as the vanishing light of the morning star. T. S. Eliot, no great enthusiast about Shelley, greatly admired such passages. Compare A. E. Housman's admiration for George Darley's description of the sea (pp. 58–9).

I bring fresh showers for the thirsting flowers,
    From the seas and the streams;
I bear light shade for the leaves when laid
    In their noon-day dreams.
From my wings are shaken the dews that waken
    The sweet buds every one,
When rocked to rest on their mother's breast,
    As she dances about the sun.
I wield the flail of the lashing hail,
    And whiten the green plains under,
And then again I dissolve it in rain,
    And laugh as I pass in thunder.

I sift the snow on the mountains below,
    And their great pines groan aghast
And all the night 'tis my pillow white,
    While I sleep in the arms of the blast.
Sublime on the towers of my skiey bowers,
    Lightning my pilot sits;
In a cavern under is fettered the thunder,
    It struggles and howls at fits;

Over earth and ocean, with gentle motion,
  This pilot is guiding me,
Lured by the love of the genii that move
  In the depths of the purple sea;
Over the rills, and the crags, and the hills,
  Over the lakes and the plains,
Wherever he dream, under mountain or stream,
  The Spirit he loves remains;
And I all the while bask in heaven's blue smile,
  Whilst he is dissolving in rains.

The sanguine sunrise, with his meteor eyes,
  And his burning plumes outspread,
Leaps on the back of my sailing rack,
  When the morning star shines dead,
As on the jag of a mountain crag,
  Which an earthquake rocks and swings,
An eagle alit one moment may sit
  In the light of its golden wings.
And when sunset may breathe, from the lit sea beneath,
  Its ardours of rest and of love,
And the crimson pall of eve may fall
  From the depth of heaven above,
With wings folded I rest, on mine airy nest,
  As still as a brooding dove.

That orbèd maiden with white fire laden,
  Whom mortals call the moon,
Glides glimmering o'er my fleece-like floor,
  By the midnight breezes strewn;
And wherever the beat of her unseen feet,
  Which only the angels hear,
May have broken the woof of my tent's thin roof,
  The stars peep behind her and peer;
And I laugh to see them whirl and flee,
  Like a swarm of golden bees,
When I widen the rent in my wind-built tent,

Till the calm rivers, lakes, and seas,
Like strips of the sky fallen through me on high,
  Are each paved with the moon and these.

I bind the sun's throne with the burning zone,
  And the moon's with a girdle of pearl;
The volcanos are dim, and the stars reel and swim,
  When the whirlwinds my banner unfurl.
From cape to cape, with a bridge-like shape,
  Over a torrent sea,
Sunbeam-proof, I hang like a roof,
  The mountains its columns be.
The triumphal arch through which I march
  With hurricane, fire, and snow,
When the powers of the air are chained to my chair,
  Is the million-coloured bow;
The sphere-fire above its soft colours wove,
  While the moist earth was laughing below.

I am the daughter of earth and water,
  And the nursling of the sky;
I pass through the pores of the ocean and shores;
  I change, but I cannot die.
For after the rain when, with never a stain,
  The pavilion of heaven is bare,
And the winds and sunbeams with their convex gleams
  Build up the blue dome of air,
I silently laugh at my own cenotaph,
  And out of the caverns of rain
Like a child from the womb, like a ghost from the tomb,
  I arise and unbuild it again.

'A Luncheon'
(Thomas Hardy Entertains the Prince of Wales)
by Max Beerbohm (1872–1956)

Max Beerbohm's great gift was for gentle, though extremely penetrating and funny, observation of the comedy of style. He sends up the Oxford Style in Zuleika Dobson *(1911), and he brings out the comedy of Hardy's in this altogether charming poem which I'm sure Hardy would have enjoyed had he read it.*

('Unglad' is an immortal verbal creation in Hardy's manner, and the beginning of the second verse exactly hits off the owlish solemnity which almost had a kind of disconcerting twinkle in it.)

Beerbohm once produced a perfect parody line for W. B. Yeats' early poetry. He said that a schoolfriend was laboriously translating some Greek classic, and came out with 'a tear shall lead the blind man'. The schoolmaster merely raised his eyes to heaven, and said, 'Clever tear.'

Lift latch, step in, be welcome, Sir,
Albeit to see you I'm unglad
And your face is fraught with a deathly shyness
Bleaching what pink it may have had,
Come in, come in, Your Royal Highness.

Beautiful weather? – Sir, that's true,
Though the farmers are casting rueful looks
At tilth's and pasture's dearth of spryness. –
Yes, Sir, I've written several books. –
A little more chicken, Your Royal Highness?

Lift latch, step out, your car is there,
To bear you hence from this antient vale.
We are both of us aged by our strange brief nighness,
But each of us lives to tell the tale.
Farewell, farewell, Your Royal Highness.

'The Self-Unseeing'
by Thomas Hardy
(1840–1928)

Hardy at his most moving, and also at his most cannily perceptive. When children are really most happy, and indeed when grown-ups are too, they are very seldom aware of the fact. Perfect happiness is not a state in which self-awareness plays a part.

Here is the ancient floor,
Footworn and hollowed and thin,
Here was the former door
Where the dead feet walked in.

She sat here in her chair,
Smiling into the fire;
He who played stood there,
Bowing it higher and higher.

Childlike, I danced in a dream;
Blessings emblazoned that day;
Everything glowed with a gleam;
Yet we were looking away!

From *David Copperfield* (1849–50)
by Charles Dickens
(1812–70)

Brooks of Sheffield is one of Dickens' best creations, in some way just as much alive as the real people in the book. No wonder David believed in Brooks, nor, strikingly enough, is there anything truly malicious about the way the gentlemen make game of him, even though we already intuit what an ugly customer Mr Murdstone may be.

We went to an hotel by the sea, where two gentlemen were smoking cigars in a room by themselves. Each of them was lying on at least four chairs, and had a large rough jacket on. In a corner was a heap of coats and boatcloaks, and a flag, all bundled up together.

They both rolled on to their feet, in an untidy sort of manner, when we came in, and said, 'Halloa, Murdstone! We thought you were dead!'

'Not yet,' said Mr Murdstone.

'And who's this shaver?' said one of the gentlemen, taking hold of me.

'That's Davy,' returned Mr Murdstone.

'Davy who?' said the gentleman. 'Jones?'

'Copperfield,' said Mr Murdstone.

'What! Bewitching Mrs Copperfield's incumbrance?' cried the gentleman. 'The pretty little widow?'

'Quinion,' said Mr Murdstone, 'take care, if you please. Somebody's sharp.'

'Who is?' asked the gentleman, laughing.

I looked up, quickly; being curious to know.

'Only Brooks of Sheffield,' said Mr Murdstone.

I was quite relieved to find that it was only Brooks of Sheffield; for, at first, I really thought it was I.

There seemed to be something very comical in the reputation of Mr Brooks of Sheffield, for both the gentlemen laughed heartily when he was mentioned, and Mr Murdstone was a good deal amused also. After some laughing, the gentleman whom he had called Quinion said:

'And what is the opinion of Brooks of Sheffield, in reference to the projected business?'

'Why, I don't know that Brooks understands much about it at present, replied Mr Murdstone; 'but he is not generally favourable, I believe.'

There was more laughter at this, and Mr Quinion said he would ring the bell for some sherry in which to drink to Brooks. This he did; and when the wine came, he made me have a little, with a biscuit, and before I drank it, stand up and say, 'Confusion to Brooks of Sheffield!' The toast was received with great applause, and such hearty laughter that it made me laugh too; at which they laughed the more. In short, we quite enjoyed ourselves.

'The Round'
by Walter de la Mare
(1873–1956)

Walter de la Mare is still widely read for a handful of poems. 'The Round' is not one of them, but there's something about it which has lodged firmly in my mind, and I have remained very fond of it.

I watched, upon a vase's rim,
An earwig – strayed from honeyed cell –
Circling a track once strange to him,
   But now known far too well.

With vexed antennae, searching space,
And giddy grope to left and right,
On – and still on – he pressed apace,
   Out of, and into, sight.

In circumambulation drear,
He neither wavered, paused nor stayed;
But now kind Providence drew near –
   A slip of wood I laid

Across his track. He scaled its edge:
And soon was safely restored to where
A sappy, dew-bright, flowering hedge
   Of dahlias greened the air.

Ay, and as apt may be my fate! . . .
Smiling, I turned to work again:
But shivered, where in shade I sate,
   And idle did remain.

'The Children of Stare'
by Walter de la Mare
(1873–1956)

De la Mare wrote much for children, but he seems to have thought them as sinister as they were attractive, if this striking poem, 'The Children of Stare', is anything to go by.

Winter is fallen early
On the house of Stare;
Birds in reverberating flocks
Haunt its ancestral box;
Bright are the plenteous berries
In clusters in the air.

Still is the fountain's music,
The dark pool icy still,
Whereupon a small and sanguine sun
Floats in a mirror on,
Into a West of crimson,
From a South of daffodil.

'Tis strange to see young children
In such a wintry house;
Like rabbits' on the frozen snow
Their tell-tale footprints go;
Their laughter rings like timbrels
'Neath evening ominous:

Their small and heightened faces
Like wine-red winter buds;
Their frolic bodies gentle as
Flakes in the air that pass,
Frail as the twirling petal
From the briar of the woods.

Above them silence lours,
   Still as an arctic sea;
Light fails; night falls; the wintry moon
   Glitters; the crocus soon
   Will open grey and distracted
   On earth's austerity:

Thick mystery, wild peril,
   Law like an iron rod: –
Yet sport they on in Spring's attire,
   Each with his tiny fire
   Blown to a core of ardour
   By the awful breath of God.

'The Snowman'

by Wallace Stevens (1879–1955)

Wallace Stevens appeals to the philosophically minded reader because many of his seemingly most ambitious poems, particularly the longer ones, seem to be not so much themselves as poems, as arguments concerning the possibility of becoming themselves.

On the other hand, Stevens can write quite different kinds of poems, not in the least concerned with themselves, poems that exactly fill Archibald Macleish's argument in Ars Poetica *that 'a poem should not mean/But be', and which keep the reader transfixed upon an object, like a snowman and an intent vision of an American winter.*

One must have a mind of winter
To regard the frost and the boughs
Of the pine-trees crusted with snow;

And have been cold a long time
To behold the junipers shagged with ice,
The spruces rough in the distant glitter

Of the January sun; and not to think
Of any misery in the sound of the wind,
In the sound of a few leaves,

Which is the sound of the land
Full of the same wind
That is blowing in the same bare place

For the listener, who listens in the snow,
And, nothing himself, beholds
Nothing that is not there and the nothing that is.

These short – very short – poems by **William Blake** *(1757–1827) have a magic like no one else's. His long poems are also magical, but to most readers inevitably boring. They have to be understood, up to a point at least, whereas these short ones do not. They are. What is there to say about the Tyger?*

'The Sick Rose'

O rose, thou art sick;
The invisible worm
That flies in the night,
In the howling storm,
Hath found out thy bed
Of crimson joy,
And her dark secret love
Does thy life destroy.

'Morning'

To find the western path,
Right through the gates of wrath
I urge my way.
Sweet mercy leads me on
With soft repentant moan;
I see the break of day.

The war of swords and spears
Melted by dewy tears
Exhales on high;
The sun is freed from fears,
And with soft grateful tears
Ascends the sky.

'To the Accuser
Who is the God of this World'

Truly, my Satan, thou art but a dunce
And dost not know the garment from the man:
Every harlot was a virgin once,
Nor canst thou ever change Kate into Nan.

Though thou art worshipped by the names divine
Of Jesus and Jehovah thou art still
The Son of Morn in weary night's decline,
The lost traveller's dream under the hill.

'The Tyger'

Tyger! Tyger! burning bright
In the forests of the night,
What immortal hand or eye
Could frame thy fearful symmetry?

In what distant deeps or skies
Burnt the fire of thine eyes?
On what wings dare he aspire?
What the hand dare sieze the fire?

And what shoulder, & what art,
Could twist the sinews of thy heart?
And when thy heart began to beat,
What dread hand? & what dread feet?

What the hammer? what the chain?
In what furnace was thy brain?
What the anvil? what dread grasp
Dare its deadly terrors clasp?

When the stars threw down their spears,
And water'd heaven with their tears,
Did he smile his work to see?
Did he who made the Lamb make thee?

Tyger! Tyger! burning bright
In the forests of the night,
What immortal hand or eye,
Dare frame thy fearful symmetry?

'Mariana'
by Alfred, Lord Tennyson
(1809–92)

The most extraordinary picture of loneliness and abandonment in English poetry. 'Mariana' is the Shakespearian heroine from Measure for Measure *who was abandoned in a country house by her betrothed, the faithless Angelo.*

> Mariana in the moated grange.
> – MEASURE FOR MEASURE

With blackest moss the flower-plots
    Were thickly crusted, one and all;
The rusted nails fell from the knots
    That held the pear to the gable-wall.
The broken sheds look'd sad and strange:
    Unlifted was the clinking latch;
    Weeded and worn the ancient thatch
Upon the lonely moated grange.
        She only said, 'My life is dreary,
           He cometh not,' she said;
        She said, 'I am aweary, aweary,
           I would that I were dead!'

Her tears fell with the dews at even;
    Her tears fell ere the dews were dried
She could not look on the sweet heaven,
    Either at morn or eventide.
After the flitting of the bats,
    When thickest dark did trance the sky,
    She drew her casement-curtain by,
And glanced athwart the glooming flats.

She only said, 'The night is dreary,
    He cometh not,' she said;
She said, 'I am aweary, aweary,
    I would that I were dead!'

Upon the middle of the night,
    Waking she heard the night-fowl crow;
The cock sung out an hour ere light;
    From the dark fen the oxen's low
Came to her; without hope of change,
    In sleep she seem'd to walk forlorn,
    Till cold winds woke the gray-eyed morn
About the lonely moated grange.
    She only said, 'The day is dreary,
        He cometh not,' she said;
    She said, 'I am aweary, aweary,
        I would that I were dead!'

About a stone-cast from the wall
    A sluice with blacken'd waters slept,
And o'er it many, round and small
    The cluster'd marish-mosses crept.
Hard by a poplar shook alway,
    All silver-green with gnarled bark:
    For leagues no other tree did mark
The level waste, the rounding gray.
    She only said, 'My life is dreary,
        He cometh not,' she said;
    She said, 'I am aweary, aweary,
        I would that I were dead!'

And ever when the moon was low
    And the shrill winds were up and away,
In the white curtain, to and fro,
    She saw the gusty shadow sway.
But when the moon was very low,
    And wild winds bound within their cell

The shadow of the poplar fell
Upon her bed, across her brow.
 She only said, 'The night is dreary,
  He cometh not,' she said;
 She said, 'I am aweary, aweary
  I would that I were dead!'

All day within the dreamy house,
 The doors upon their hinges creak'd;
The blue fly sung in the pane; the mouse
 Behind the mouldering wainscot shriek'd
Or from the crevice peer'd about.
 Old faces glimmer'd thro' the doors,
 Old footsteps trod the upper floors,
Old voices called her from without.
 She only said, 'My life is dreary,
  He cometh not,' she said;
 She said, 'I am aweary, aweary,
  I would that I were dead!'

The sparrow's chirrup on the roof,
 The slow clock ticking, and the sound
Which to the wooing wind aloof
 The poplar made, did all confound
Her sense; but most she loathed the hour
 When the thick-moted sunbeam lay
 Athwart the chambers, and the day
Was sloping toward his western bower.
 Then said she, 'I am very dreary,
  He will not come,' she said;
 She wept, 'I am aweary, aweary,
  O God, that I were dead!'

'La Figlia Che Piange'
by T. S. Eliot (1888–1965)

This poem, one of Eliot's early ones, is a marvellous mixture of selfishness and wistful longing: both presented in an aesthetic frame and as a matter of aesthetic enjoyment to the speaker.

O quam te memorem virgo . . .

Stand on the highest pavement of the stair –
Lean on a garden urn –
Weave, weave the sunlight in your hair –
Clasp your flowers to you with a pained surprise –
Fling them to the ground and turn
With a fugitive resentment in your eyes:
But weave, weave the sunlight in your hair.

So I would have had him leave,
So I would have had her stand and grieve,
So he would have left
As the soul leaves the body torn and bruised,
As the mind deserts the body it has used.
I should find
Some way incomparably light and deft,
Some way we both should understand,
Simple and faithless as a smile and shake of the hand.

She turned away, but with the autumn weather
Compelled my imagination many days,
Many days and many hours:
Her hair over her arms and her arms full of flowers.
And I wonder how they should have been together!
I should have lost a gesture and a pose.
Sometimes these cogitations still amaze
The troubled midnight and the noon's repose.

– 21 –

'How to Get On in Society'
by John Betjeman (1906–84)

Inspired by Nancy Mitford's piece on 'U and Non-U' usage, itself based on the research of a scholarly philologist, the charm of this poem consists in making happily ridiculous the whole question of what is and is not 'done'. A serious snob would consider it in bad taste or merely silly.

Betjeman is incapable of satire, but his sense of comedy and his nostalgia for the past are unique and like nothing else in the world of poetry. He loves the Victorians, just as he loves Perivale and Camberley and the natives who live there, but the lyric world he creates could only be Betjeman and nothing else.

Phone for the fish-knives, Norman
    As Cook is a little unnerved;
You kiddies have crumpled the serviettes
    And I must have things daintily served.

Are the requisites all in the toilet?
    The frills round the cutlets can wait
Till the girl has replenished the cruets
    And switched on the logs in the grate.

It's ever so close in the lounge, dear,
    But the vestibule's comfy for tea
And Howard is out riding on horseback
    So do come and take some with me.

Now here is a fork for your pastries
    And do use the couch for your feet;
I know what I wanted to ask you –
    Is trifle sufficient for sweet?

Milk and then just as it comes dear?
    I'm afraid the preserve's full of stones;
Beg pardon, I'm soiling the doileys
    With afternoon tea-cakes and scones.

'A Song of a Young Lady to Her Ancient Lover'
by Lord Rochester
(1647–80)

The ancient person was probably no more than 45. Rakes and dissipated young men, as Rochester certainly was, thought of themselves as completely worn out at an age which people today would consider the prime of life. The poem has a pleasing irony and contrives to persuade us that the young lady who speaks really was in love with him, and feels for him just as she says.

Ancient person, for whom I
All the flattering youth defy,
Long be it ere thou grow old,
Aching, shaking, crazy, cold;
   But still continue as thou art,
   Ancient person of my heart.

On thy withered lips and dry,
Which like barren furrows lie,
Brooding kisses I will pour
Shall thy youthful [heat] restore
(Such kind showers in autumn fall,
And a second spring recall);
   Nor from thee will ever part,
   Ancient person of my heart.

Thy nobler part, which but to name
In our sex would be counted shame,
By age's frozen grasp possessed,
From [his] ice shall be released,
And soothed by my reviving hand,
In former warmth and vigor stand.
All a lover's wish can reach
For thy joy my love shall teach,

And for thy pleasure shall improve
All that art can add to love.
   Yet still I love thee without art,
   Ancient person of my heart.

'Love and Life'

All my past life is mine no more;
   The flying hours are gone,
Like transitory dreams given o'er
Whose images are kept in store
   By memory alone.

Whatever is to come is not:
   How can it then be mine?
The present moment's all my lot,
And that, as fast as it is got,
   Phyllis, is wholly thine.

Then talk not of inconstancy,
   False hearts, and broken vows;
If I, by miracle, can be
This livelong minute true to thee,'
   'Tis all that heaven allows.

'Say Not the Struggle Naught Availeth'
by Arthur Hugh Clough
(1819–61)

Winston Churchill unexpectedly popularized this poem in 1942 when he recited it on the radio in the course of one of his rousing speeches. It is indeed a remarkably memorable poem which gains on one each time one reads it, and the images have a kind of weird compulsive charm as if they were in constant movement, as if in battle for life. Clough died of consumption and Swinburne wrote rather unkindly about him, 'There was once a poet called Clough/Who his friends all wanted to puff./But the public, though dull/hasn't quite such a skull,/As belongs to believers in Clough.' Clough's reputation in fact vanished entirely, and has only been revived in living memory.

Say not, the struggle nought availeth,
    The labour and the wounds are vain,
The enemy faints not, nor faileth,
    And as things have been they remain.

If hopes were dupes, fears may be liars;
    It may be, in yon smoke concealed,
Your comrades chase e'en now the fliers,
    And, but for you, possess the field.

For while the tired waves, vainly breaking,
    Seem here no painful inch to gain,
Far back, through creeks and inlets making,
    Comes silent, flooding in, the main,

And not by eastern windows only,
    When daylight comes, comes in the light,
In front, the sun climbs slow, how slowly,
    But westward, look, the land is bright.

E. M. Forster (1879–1970) on Jane Austen
from *Abinger Harvest*
(1936)

A distinctly feline novelist makes some shrewd comments on a much greater one. But the comments are shrewd, and Jane Austen herself would have appreciated them.

Some readers find the triviality [of Jane Austen's letters] delightful, and rightly point out that there is a charm in little things. Yes, when it is the charm of Cowper. But the little things must hold out their little hands to one another; and here there is a scrappiness which prevents even tartness from telling. This brings us to the heart of the matter, to Miss Austen's fundamental weakness as a letter-writer. She has not enough subject matter on which to exercise her powers. Her character and sex as well as her environment removed her from public affairs, and she was too sincere and spontaneous to affect any interest which she did not feel. She takes no account of politics or religion, and none of the war except when it brings prize-money to her brothers. Her comments on literature are provincial and perfunctory – with one exception, and a significant one, which we shall cite in a moment. When she writes a letter she has nothing in her mind except the wish to tell her sister everything; and so she flits from the cows to the currant bushes, from the currant bushes to Mrs Hall of Sherborne, gives Mrs Hall a tap, and flits back again. She suffers from a poverty of material which did no injury to the novels, and indeed contributes to their triumph. Miss Bates may flit and Mrs Norris tap as much as they like, because they do so inside a frame which has been provided by a great artist, and Meryton may reproduce the atmosphere of Steventon because it imports something else – some alignment not to be found on any map. The letters lack direction. What an improvement when she is startled, an elm falls, they have to go to the dentist! Then her powers of description find fuller play, and to the affection which she always feels for her correspondents she adds concentration, and an interest in the subject-matter.

The improvement becomes more noticeable in the second volume, that is to say after 1811. She had received a series of pleasant surprises. Her novels, which had always found favour in private readings, began to get published and gain wider audiences. Warren Hastings admired them, and *Emma* was dedicated to the Prince Regent shortly after his victory at Waterloo. She went to London oftener, perhaps saw Mr Crabbe in the distance, and had a note from Mrs Hannah More. While rating these joys at their proper worth, she could not but gain the notion of a more amusing and varied world; and perhaps she is one of the few country writers whom wider experience and consort with the literary would not have ruined.

Meanwhile her success reacted on her family. Her seven brothers (with the exception of a mysterious George who is never mentioned), her sister, her sisters-in-law, her nephews and, most of all, her nieces were deeply impressed. One of the nieces, Anna, took to scribbling on her own, and sent Aunt Jane from time to time instalments of a novel to read aloud to Aunt Cassandra. Miss Austen's replies are admirable. She is stimulated because the writer is a relation, and she pours out helpful criticisms, all put in a kindly, easy way. Most of them are connected with 'getting things right' – always a preoccupation with English novelists, from Defoe to Arnold Bennett. Times, places, and probabilities must be considered, but Anna must beware of copying life slavishly, for life sometimes gets things wrong:

> I have scratched out Sir Thos: from walking with the other Men to the Stables &ct the very day after breaking his arm – for though I and your Papa *did* walk out immediately after his arm was set, I think it can be so little usual as to *appear* unnatural in a book – & it does not seem to be material that Sir Thos: should go with them. Lyme will not do. Lyme is towards 40 miles distant from Dawlish & would not be

talked of there. – I have put Starcross instead. If you prefer *Exeter*, that must be always safe.

Thursday. We finished it last night, after our return from drinking tea at the Gt House. – The last chapter does not please us so well, we do not thoroughly like the *Play*: perhaps from having had too much of Plays in that way lately. And we think you had better not leave England. Let the Portmans go to Ireland, but as you know nothing of the Manners there you had better not go with them. You will be in danger of giving false representations. Stick to Bath and the Foresters. There you will be quite at home. – Your Aunt C. does not like desultory novels and is rather fearful yours will be too much so, that there will be too frequently a change from one set of people to another, & that circumstances will be sometimes introduced of apparent consequence, which will lead to nothing. – It will not be so great an objection to *me*, if it does. I allow much more Latitude than she does – & think Nature and Spirit cover many sins of a wandering story.

Here, again, the English school of fiction speaks, and puts its case amiably and privately, as it should. Manifestoes belong to abroad. Aunt Cassandra likes a book to be neat and tidy: Aunt Jane does not much mind. And Anna, receiving these letters, in which detailed comment is mixed with sound generalizations, must have been delighted; she must have found her novel much better than she thought and yet been stimulated to correct in it what was wrong. We share the enthusiasm. It sounds a lovely novel, and we turn to the terminal notes to see what more Mr Chapman has to tell us about it. Alas; he can tell us too much:

The story to which most of these letters of Aunt Jane's refer was never finished. It was laid aside because my mother's hands were so full . . . The story was laid by for years, and then one day in a fit of despondency burnt. I remember sitting on the rug and watching its destruction, amused with the flames and the sparks which kept breaking out in the blackened paper.

Thus writes Anna's daughter; and Anna's novel, with the Portmans and Foresters, who seemed so fascinating, has gone up the chimney for ever. But the tiny flicker of light which it casts backwards is valuable. We see Miss Austen and Jane Austen for a moment as one person. The letter-writer and the novelist have fused, because a letter is being written to a niece about a novel. Family feeling has done the trick; and, after all, whatever opinion we hold about her, we must agree that the supreme thing in life to her was the family. She knew no other allegiance; if there was an early love affair in the west of England, and if her lover died, as did her sister Cassandra's, she never clung to his memory, unless she utilizes it in *Persuasion*. Intimacy out of the unknown never overwhelmed her. No single person ever claimed her. She was part of a family, and her dearest Cassandra only the dearest in that family. The family was the unit within which her heart had liberty of choice; friends, neighbours, plays and fame were all objects to be picked up in the course of a flight outside and brought back to the nest for examination. They often laughed over the alien trophies, for they were a hard humorous family. And these letters, however we judge them on their own count, are invaluable as a document. They show, more clearly than ever, that Miss Austen was part of the Austens, the Knights, the Leighs, the Lefroys. The accidents of birth and relationship were more sacred to her than anything else in the world, and she introduced this faith as the groundwork of her six great novels.

'Nothing to Fear'
by Kingsley Amis
(1922–95)

*Amis was equally versatile as a novelist, poet, and letter-writer –
indeed a virtuoso of all three forms – although his poems are not the
equal of Larkin's poems in a similar style. His fear of death was as
overwhelming as his appetite for sex, and he dramatizes both in his
own exuberant way in this poem.*

All fixed: early arrival at the flat
Lent by a friend, whose note says *Lucky sod*;
Drinks on the tray; the cover-story pat
And quite uncheckable; her husband off
Somewhere with all the kids till six o'clock
(Which ought to be quite long enough);
And all worth while: face really beautiful,
Good legs and hips, and as for breasts – my God.
What about guilt, compunction and such stuff?
I've had my fill of all that cock;
It'll wear off, as usual.

Yes, all fixed. Then why this slight trembling,
Dry mouth, quick pulse-rate, sweaty hands,
As though she were the first? No, not impatience,
Nor fear of failure, thank you, Jack.
Beauty, they tell me, is a dangerous thing,
Whose touch will burn, but I'm asbestos, see?
All worth while – it's a dead coincidence
That sitting here, a bag of glands
Tuned up to concert pitch, I seem to sense
A different style of caller at my back,
As cold as ice, but just as set on me.

'The Fish'

by Elizabeth Bishop

(1911–79)

The poem does give one a remarkable feeling of 'fishness' (compare the Victorian T. E. Browne trying to imagine what it might be like to be a cod, p. 71). Perhaps the end is a bit too much of a pat on the back for the poet? And, as a critic remarked, the fish might have been excused for muttering, 'Thank you for nothing, lady', when she finally let him off the hook.

I caught a tremendous fish
and held him beside the boat
half out of water, with my hook
fast in a corner of his mouth.
He didn't fight.
He hadn't fought at all.
He hung a grunting weight,
battered and venerable
and homely. Here and there
his brown skin hung in strips
like ancient wallpaper,
and its pattern of darker brown
was like wallpaper;
shapes like full-blown roses
stained and lost through age.
He was speckled with barnacles,
fine rosettes of lime,
and infested
with tiny white sea-lice,
and underneath two or three
rags of green weed hung down.
While his gills were breathing in
the terrible oxygen
– the frightening gills,

fresh and crisp with blood,
that can cut so badly –
I thought of the coarse white flesh
packed in like feathers,
the big bones and the little bones,
the dramatic reds and blacks
of his shiny entrails,
and the pink swim-bladder
like a big peony.
I looked into his eyes
which were far larger than mine
but shallower, and yellowed,
the irises backed and packed
with tarnished tinfoil
seen through the lenses
of old scratched isinglass.

They shifted a little, but not
to return my stare.
– It was more like the tipping
of an object toward the light.
I admired his sullen face,
the mechanism of his jaw,
and then I saw
that from his lower lip
– if you could call it a lip –
grim, wet, and weaponlike,
hung five old pieces of fish-line,
or four and a wire leader
with the swivel still attached,
with all their five big hooks
grown firmly in his mouth.
A green line, frayed at the end
where he broke it, two heavier lines,
and a fine black thread
still crimped from the strain and snap
when it broke and he got away.

Like medals with their ribbons
frayed and wavering,
a five-haired beard of wisdom
trailing from his aching jaw.
I stared and stared
and victory filled up
the little rented boat,
from the pool of bilge
where oil had spread a rainbow
around the rusted engine
to the bailer rusted orange,
the sun-cracked thwarts,
the oarlocks on their strings,
the gunnels – until everything
was rainbow, rainbow, rainbow!
And I let the fish go.

'The Kiss'
by Coventry Patmore
(1823–96)

Coventry Patmore is a man of many moods. He can be very sentimental, though often effectively so, in the Victorian manner; but this charming verse shows him in his dry, light and sardonic mood, well aware that every Angel in the House has her own strategies and her own lack of scruple.

The long poem, 'The Angel in the House' has many colourful and tender moments, including this description.

'I saw you take his kiss!' ''Tis true.'
'O, modesty!' ''Twas strictly kept:
'He thought me asleep; at least, I knew
'He thought I thought he thought I slept.'

From 'The Angel in the House'

A voice, the sweeter for the grace
   Of suddenness, while thus I dream'd,
'Good-morning!' said or sang. Her face
   The mirror of the morning seem'd.
Her sisters in the garden walk'd,
   And would I come? Across the Hall
She took me; and we laugh'd and talk'd
   About the Flower-show, and the Ball.
Their pinks had won a spade for prize:
   But that was gallantly withdrawn
For 'Jones on Wiltshire Butterflies:'
   How rude! And so we paced the lawn,
Close-cut, and, with geranium-plots,
   A rival glow of green and red;
Then counted sixty apricots
   On one small tree. The goldfish fed

And watched where black with scarlet tans
    Proud Psyche stood and flashed like flame
Showing and shutting splendid fans,
    And in the prize we found its name
And I rode slow 'tward home, my breast
    A load of joy and tender care:
And this delight, which life oppress'd,
    To fix'd aims grew, that ask'd for pray'r:
And I reach'd home, where, whip in hand
    And soil'd bank-notes all ready, stood
The Farmer who farm'd all my land,
    Except the little Park and Wood.
And, with the accustom'd compliment
    Of talk, and beef, and frothing beer,
I, my own steward, took my rent,
    Three hundred pounds for half the year:
Our witnesses the Maid and Groom,
    We sign'd the lease for seven years more,
And bade Good-day. Then to my room
    I went, and closed and lock'd the door,
And cast myself down on my bed,
    And there, with many a blissful tear,
I vow'd to love and pray'd to wed
    The Maiden who had grown so dear;
Thank'd God who had set her in my path;
    And promised, as I hoped to win,
I never would sully my faith
    By the least selfishness or sin;
Whatever in her sight I'd seem
    I'd really be; I'd never blend
With my delight in her a dream
    'Twould change her cheek to comprehend;
And, if she wish'd it, I'd prefer
    Another's to my own success;
And always seek the best for her,
    With unofficious tenderness.

'At Her Window'
by Frederick Locker-Lampson
(1821–95)

*Locker-Lampson's delightful poem is written in exactly the same spirit
as John Betjeman's immortal 'Miss Joan Hunter Dunn'. The Victorians could send themselves and their society up in much the same way as
Betjeman sent up the habits and inhabitants of 1930s culture.*

*George Meredith was a very prolific poet and novelist but has not
survived very well as either. But 'Love in the Valley' is not only a
charming poem, and one easily transported in the mental luggage, but
inspired, both in feeling and metre, Betjeman's outcry from an army
wife of 1930s military Surrey.*

> Beating Heart! we come again
>   Where my Love reposes:
> This is Mabel's window-pane;
>   These are Mabel's roses.
>
> Is she nested? Does she kneel
>   In the twilight stilly,
> Lily clad from throat to heel,
>   She, my virgin Lily?
>
> Soon the wan, the wistful stars,
>   Fading, will forsake her;
> Elves of light, on beamy bars,
>   Whisper then, and wake her.
>
> Let this friendly pebble plead
>   At her flowery grating;
> If she hear me will she heed?
>   *Mabel, I am waiting?*

Mabel will be deck'd anon,
  Zoned in bride's apparel;
Happy zone! O hark to yon
  Passion-shaken carol!

Sing thy song, thou trancèd thrush,
  Pipe thy best, thy clearest; −
Hush, her lattice moves, O hush −
  Dearest Mabel! − dearest . . .

'Love in the Valley'
by George Meredith
(1828–1909)

Under yonder beech-tree single on the green-sward,
  Couched with her arms behind her golden head,
Knees and tresses folded to slip and ripple idly,
  Lies my young love sleeping in the shade.
Had I the heart to slide an arm beneath her,
  Press her parting lips as her waist I gather slow,
Waking in amazement she could not but embrace me:
  Then would she hold me and never let me go?

Shy as the squirrel and wayward as the swallow,
  Swift as the swallow along the river's light
Circleting the surface to meet his mirrored winglets,
  Fleeter she seems in her stay than in her flight.
Shy as the squirrel that leaps among the pine-tops,
  Wayward as the swallow overhead at set of sun,
She whom I love is hard to catch and conquer,
  Hard, but O the glory of the winning were she won!

When her rnother tends her before the laughing mirror,
    Tying up her laces, looping up her hair,
Often she thinks, were this wild thing wedded,
    More love should I have, and much less care.
When her mother tends her before the lighted mirror,
    Loosening her laces, combing down her curls,
Often she thinks, were this wild thing wedded,
    I should miss but one for many boys and girls.

Heartless she is as the shadow in the meadows
    Fling to the hills on a blue and breezy noon.
No, she is athirst and drinking up her wonder:
    Earth to her is young as the slip of the new moon.
Deals she an unkindness, 'tis but her rapid measure,
    Even as in a dance; and her smile can heal no less:
Like the swinging May-cloud that pelts the flowers with
        hailstones
    Off a sunny border, she was made to bruise and bless.

Lovely are the curves of the white owl sweeping
    Wavy in the dusk lit by one large star.
Lone on the fir-branch, his rattle-note unvaried,
    Brooding o'er the gloom, spins the brown eve-jar.
Darker grows the valley, more and more forgetting:
    So were it with me if forgetting could be willed.
Tell the grassy hollow that holds the bubbling well-spring,
    Tell it to forget the source that keeps it filled.

Stepping down the hill with her fair companions,
    Arm in arm, all against the raying West,
Boldly she sings, to the merry tune she marches,
    Brave in her shape, and sweeter unpossessed.
Sweeter, for she is what my heart first awaking
    Whispered the world was; morning light is she.
Love that so desires would fain keep her changeless;
    Fain would fling the net, and fain have her free.

Happy happy time, when the white star hovers
   Low over dim fields fresh with bloomy dew,
Near the face of dawn, that draws athwart the darkness,
   Threading it with colour, as yewberries the yew.
Thicker crowd the shades as the grave East deepens
   Glowing, and with crimson a long cloud swells.
Maiden still the morn is; and strange she is, and secret;
   Strange her eyes; her cheeks are cold as cold sea-shells.

Mother of the dews, dark eye-lashed twilight,
   Low-lidded twilight, o'er the valley's brim,
Rounding on thy breast sings the dew-delighted skylark,
   Clear as though the dewdrops had their voice in him.
Hidden where the rose-flush drinks the rayless planet,
   Fountain-full he pours the spraying fountain-showers.
Let me hear her laughter, I would have her ever
   Cool as dew in twilight, the lark above the flowers.

All the girls are out with their baskets for the primrose;
   Up lanes, woods through, they troop in joyful bands.
My sweet leads: she knows not why, but now she loiters,
   Eyes the bent anemones, and hangs her hands.
Such a look will tell that the violets are peeping,
   Coming the rose: and unaware a cry
Springs in her bosom for odours and for colour,
   Covert and the nightingale; she knows not why.

Hither she comes; she comes to me; she lingers,
   Deepens her brown eyebrows, while in new surprise
High rise the lashes in wonder of a stranger;
   Yet am I the light and living of her eyes.
Something friends have told her fills her heart to
      brimming,
Nets her in her blushes, and wounds her, and tames. –
Sure of her haven, O like a dove alighting,
   Arms up, she dropped: our souls were in our names.

Could I find a place to be alone with heaven,
  I would speak my heart out: heaven is my need.
Every woodland tree is flushing like the dogwood,
  Flashing like the whitebeam, swaying like the reed.
Flushing like the dogwood crimson in October;
  Streaming like the flag-reed South-West blown;
Flashing as in gusts the sudden-lighted whitebeam:
  All seem to know what is for heaven alone.

'Love in a Valley'
by John Betjeman
(1906–84)

Take me, Lieutenant, to that Surrey homestead!
  Red comes the winter and your rakish car,
Red among the hawthorns, redder than the hawberries
  And trails of old man's nuisance, and noisier far.
Far, far below me roll the Coulsdon woodlands,
  White down the valley curves the living rail,[1]
Tall, tall, above me, olive spike the pinewoods,
  Olive against blue-black, moving in the gale.

Deep down the drive go the cushioned rhododendrons,
  Deep down, sand deep, drives the heather root,
Deep the spliced timber barked around the summer-house,
  Light lies the tennis-court, plantain underfoot.
What a winter welcome to what a Surrey homestead!
  Oh! the metal lantern and white enamelled door!
Oh! the spread of orange from the gas-fire on the carpet!
  Oh! the tiny patter, sandalled footsteps on the floor!

[1] Southern Electric 25 mins.

Fling wide the curtains! – that's a Surrey sunset
    Low down the line sings the Addiscombe train,
Leaded are the windows lozenging the crimson,
    Drained dark the pines in resin-scented rain.
Portable Lieutenant! they carry you to China
    And me to lonely shopping in a brilliant arcade;
Firm hand, fond hand, switch the giddy engine!
    So for us a last time is bright light made.

'Marriage'
by Marianne Moore
(1887–1972)

Anthony Powell observed that there is only one way of finding out what marriage is like: 'Get married, nothing else will quite do.' Marianne Moore never did try, but that seems to make her ruminations on the metaphysical state of matrimony all the more disconcerting, and illuminating.

This institution,
perhaps one should say enterprise
out of respect for which
one says one need not change one's mind
about a thing one has believed in,
requiring public promises
of one's intention
to fulfil a private obligation:
I wonder what Adam and Eve
think of it by this time,
this fire-gilt steel
alive with goldenness;
how bright it shows –
'of circular traditions and impostures,
committing many spoils,'
requiring all one's criminal ingenuity
to avoid!
Psychology which explains everything
explains nothing,
and we are still in doubt.
Eve: beautiful woman –
I have seen her
when she was so handsome
she gave me a start,
able to write simultaneously

in three languages –
English, German, and French –
and talk in the meantime;
equally positive in demanding a commotion
and in stipulating quiet:
'I should like to be alone';
to which the visitor replies,
'I should like to be alone;
why not be alone together?'
Below the incandescent stars
below the incandescent fruit,
the strange experience of beauty;
its existence is too much;
it tears one to pieces
and each fresh wave of consciousness
is poison.
forgetting that there is in woman
a quality of mind
which as an instinctive manifestation
is unsafe,
he goes on speaking
in a formal customary strain,
of 'past states, the present state,
seals, promises,
the evil one suffered,
the good one enjoys,
hell, heaven,
everything convenient
to promote one's joy.'
In him a state of mind
perceives what it was not
intended that he should;
'he experiences a solemn joy
in seeing that he has become an idol.'
Plagued by the nightingale
in the new leaves,
with its silence –

not its silence but its silences,
he says of it:
'It clothes me with a shirt of fire.'
'He dares not clap his hands
to make it go on
lest it should fly off;
if he does nothing, it will sleep;
if he cries out, it will not understand.'
Unnerved by the nightingale
and dazzled by the apple,
impelled by 'the illusion of a fire
effectual to extinguish fire,'
compared with which
the shining of the earth
is but deformity – a fire
'as high as deep
as bright as broad
as long as life itself,'
he stumbles over marriage,
'a very trivial object indeed'
to have destroyed the attitude
in which he stood –
'See her, see her in this common world,'
the central flaw
in that first crystal-fine experiment,
this amalgamation which can never be more
than an interesting impossibility,
describing it
as 'that strange paradise
unlike flesh, stones,
gold or stately buildings,
the choicest piece of my life:
the heart rising
in its estate of peace
as a boat rises
with the rising of the water';
constrained in speaking of the serpent –

shed snakeskin in the history of politeness
not to be returned to again –
that invaluable accident
exonerating Adam.
And he has beauty also;
it's distressing – the O thou
to whom from whom,
without whom nothing – Adam;
'something feline,
something colubrine' – how true!
a crouching mythological monster
in that Persian miniature of emerald mines,
raw silk – ivory white, snow white,
oyster white, and six others –
that paddock full of leopards and giraffes –
long lemon-yellow bodies
sown with trapezoids of blue.
Alive with words,
vibrating like a cymbal
touched before it has been struck,
he has prophesied correctly –
the industrious waterfall,
'the speedy stream
which violently bears all before it,
at one time silent as the air
and now as powerful as the wind.'
'Treading chasms
on the uncertain footing of a spear,'
and proves it to the bone,
impatient to assure you
that impatience is the mark of independence,
not of bondage.
'Married people often look that way' –
'seldom and cold, up and down,
mixed and malarial
with a good day and a bad.'
We Occidentals are so unemotional,

self lost, the irony preserved
in 'the Ahasuerus *tête-à-tête* banquet'
with its small orchids like snakes' tongues,
with its 'good monster, lead the way,'
with little laughter
and munificence of humor
in that quixotic atmosphere of frankness
in which 'four o'clock does not exist,
but at five o'clock
the ladies in their imperious humility
are ready to receive you';
in which experience attests
that men have power
and sometimes one is made to feel it.
He says, 'What monarch would not blush
to have a wife
with hair like a shaving brush?'
The fact of woman
is 'not the sound of the flute
but very poison.'
She says, 'Men are monopolists
of "stars, garters, buttons
and other shining baubles" –
unfit to be the guardians
of another person's happiness.'
He says, 'These mummies
must be handled carefully –
"the crumbs from a lion's meal,
a couple of shins and the bit of an ear";
turn to the letter M
and you will find
that "a wife is a coffin,"
that severe object
with the pleasing geometry
the ease of the philosopher
unfathered by a woman.
Unhelpful Hymen!

a kind of overgrown cupid
reduced to insignificance
by the mechanical advertising
parading as involuntary comment,
by that experiment of Adam's
with ways out but no way in –
the ritual of marriage,
augmenting all its lavishness;
its fiddlehead ferns,
lotus flowers, opuntias, white dromedaries,
its hippopotamus –
nose and mouth combined
in one magnificent hopper –
its snake and the potent apple.
He tells us
that 'for love that will
gaze an eagle blind,
that is with Hercules
climbing the trees
in the garden of the Hesperides,
from forty-five to seventy
is the best age,'
commending it
as a fine art, as an experiment,
a duty or as merely recreation.
One must not call him ruffian
nor friction a calamity –
the fight to be affectionate:
'no truth can be fully known
until it has been tried
by the tooth of disputation.'
The blue panther with black eyes,
the basalt panther with blue eyes,
entirely graceful –
one must give them the path –
the black obsidian Diana
who 'darkeneth her countenance

as a bear doth,'
the spiked hand
that has an affection for one
stipulating space not people,
refusing to be buried
and uniquely disappointing,
revengefully wrought in the attitude
of an adoring child
to a distinguished parent.'
She says, 'This butterfly,
this waterfly, this nomad
that has "proposed
to settle on my hand for life" –
What can one do with it?
There must have been more time
in Shakespeare's day
to sit and watch a play.
You know so many artists who are fools.'
He says, 'You know so many fools
who are not artists.'
The fact forgot
that 'some have merely rights
while some have obligations,'
he loves himself so much,
he can permit himself
no rival in that love.
She loves herself so much,
she cannot see herself enough –
a statuette of ivory on ivory,
the logical last touch
to an expansive splendor
earned as wages for work done:
one is not rich but poor
when one can always seem so right.
What can one do for them –
these savages
condemned to disaffect

all those who are not visionaries
alert to undertake the silly task
of making people noble?
This model of petrine fidelity
who 'leaves her peaceful husband
only because she has seen enough of him' –
that orator reminding you,
'I am yours to command.'
'Everything to do with love is mystery;
it is more than a day's work
to investigate this science.'
One sees that it is rare –
that striking grasp of opposites
opposed each to the other, not to unity,
which in cycloid inclusiveness
has dwarfed the demonstration
of Columbus with the egg –
a triumph of simplicity –
that charitive Euroclydon
of frightening disinterestedness
which the world hates,
admitting:
'I am such a cow,
if I had a sorrow
I should feel it a long time;
I am not one of those
who have a great sorrow
in the morning
and a great joy at noon';
which says: 'I have encountered it
among those unpretentious
protégés of wisdom,
where seeming to parade
as the debater and the Roman,
the statesmanship
of an archaic Daniel Webster
persists to their simplicity of temper

as the essence of the matter:
"Liberty and union
now and forever";
the Book on the writing table;
the hand in the breast pocket.'

'Marriages'
by Philip Larkin
(1922–85)

An unpublished early poem from June 1951 gives a male view of the question of marriage which is surprisingly charitable and touchingly close to the mark. An exquisite poem – why didn't he include it in his first collection?

When those of us who seem
Immodestly-accurate
Transcriptions of a dream
Are tired of singleness,
Their confidence will mate
Only with confidence –
With an equal candescence,
With a pregnant selfishness.

Not so with the remainder:
Frogmarched by old need
They chaffer for a partner –
Some undesirable,
With whom it is agreed
That words such as liberty,
Impulse, or beauty
Shall be unmentionable.

Scarecrows of chivalry.
They strike strange bargains –
Adder-faced singularity
Espouses a nailed-up childhood,
Skin-disease pardons
Soft horror of living,
A gabble is forgiven
By chronic solitude.

So they are gathered in;
So they are not wasted,
As they would have been
By intelligent rancour,
An integrity of self-hatred.
Whether they forget
What they wanted first or not
They tarnish at quiet anchor.

Part II

SOMETHING FOR THE JOURNEY

'Musée des Beaux Arts'
by W. H. Auden (1907–73)

'Memorable words' was how Auden himself defined poetry; and as he knew very well himself, the electrifying magic of his early poetry is particularly memorable. But he also had the supreme gift of expounding a thesis – in this case, the Great Painter's attitude to suffering and death – in a manner so graphic that it creates a memorable picture of its own.

About suffering they were never wrong,
The Old Masters: how well they understood
Its human position; how it takes place
While someone else is eating or opening a window or just
    walking dully along;
How, when the aged are reverently, passionately waiting
For the miraculous birth, there always must be
Children who did not specially want it to happen, skating
On a pond at the edge of the wood:
They never forgot
That even the dreadful martyrdom must run its course
Anyhow in a corner, some untidy spot
Where the dogs go on with their doggy life and the
    torturer's horse
Scratches its innocent behind on a tree.

In Breughel's *Icarus*, for instance: how everything turns
    away
Quite leisurely from the disaster; the ploughman may
Have heard the splash, the forsaken cry,
But for him it was not an important failure; the sun shone
As it had to on the white legs disappearing into the green
Water; and the expensive delicate ship that must have seen
Something amazing, a boy falling out of the sky,
Had somewhere to get to and sailed calmly on.

'A War'
by Randall Jarrell
(1914–65)

Jarrell was a brilliant critic and deliciously satiric novelist. There is a portrait of Marianne McCarthy as Gertrude in his brief Pictures from an Institution *which, once read, is never forgotten. This equally brief glimpse of what aircrews underwent in the 1939–45 war makes its point very mordantly. Jarrell himself was in the US Air Force at the time.*

There set out, slowly, for a Different World,
At four, on winter mornings, different legs . . .
You can't break eggs without making an omelette
– That's what they tell the eggs.

'Tell All the Truth But Tell It Slant'
by Emily Dickinson (1830–86)

A wonderful poet at her best; but, unlike Blake, Emily Dickinson
seldom keeps going to the end of what is always a short poem. Philip
Larkin observed that her poems sometimes seemed to make a virtue out
of collapsing, as if the weight of inspiration could no longer be borne.
That is certainly not true of either of these poems.

Tell all the Truth but tell it slant –
Success in Circuit lies
Too bright for our infirm Delight
The Truth's superb surprise
As Lightning to the Children eased
With explanation kind
The Truth must dazzle gradually
Or every man be blind –

'Safe in Their Alabaster Chambers'

Safe in their Alabaster Chambers –
Untouched by Morning
And untouched by Noon –
Sleep the meek members of the Resurrection –
Rafter of satin,
And Roof of stone.

Light laughs the breeze
In her Castle above them –
Babbles the Bee in a stolid Ear
Pipe the Sweet Birds in ignorant cadence –
Ah, what sagacity perished here!

A. E. Housman
(1885–1936)

Housman's views on poetry are always rewarding. He enjoyed Swinburne, which makes this criticism and the quotation from George Darley's unfinished poem 'Nepenthe' (1835) all the more effective.

Poetry, which in itself is simply a tone of the voice, a particular way of saying things, is mainly concerned with three great provinces. First, with human affection, and those emotions which we assign to the heart: no one could say that Swinburne succeeded or excelled in this province. The next province is the world of thought; the contemplation of life and the universe: in this province Swinburne's ideas and reflections are not indeed identical with those of Mrs Hemans, but they belong to the same intellectual order as hers: unwound from their cocoon of words they are either superficial or second-hand. Last, there is the province of external nature as perceived by our senses; and on this I must dwell for a little, because there is one department of external nature which Swinburne is supposed to have made his own: the sea.

The sea, to be sure, is a large department; and that is how it succeeded in attracting Swinburne's attention; for he seldom noticed any object of external nature unless it was very large, very brilliant, or very violently coloured. But the sea as a subject of poetry is somewhat barren. Those poets who have a true eye for nature and a sure pen for describing it, spend few words on describing the sea; and their few words describe it better than Swinburne's thousands. It is historically certain that he had seen the sea, but if it were not, it could not with certainty have been inferred from his descriptions: they might have been written by a man who had never been outside Warwickshire. Descriptions of nature equally accurate, though not equally eloquent, have actually been composed by persons blind from their birth, merely by combining anew the words

and phrases which they have had read to them from books.
When Swinburne writes thus –

> And the night was alive and anhungered of life as a
>   tiger from toils cast free:
> And a rapture of rage made joyous the spirit and
>   strength of the soul of the sea.
> All the weight of the wind bore down on it,
>   freighted with death for fraught:
> And the keen waves kindled and quickened as things
>   transfigured or things distraught.
> And madness fell on them laughing and leaping; and
>   madness came on the wind:
> And the might and the light and the darkness of
>   storm were as storm in the heart of Ind.
> Such glory, such terror, such passion, as lighten and
>   harrow the far fierce East,
> Rang, shone, spake, shuddered around us: the night
>   was an altar with death for priest –

it would be cruel to set against such a passage a single line of
Tennyson's or a single epithet of Shakespeare's: I take instead a
snatch of verse whose author few of you know and most of
you never heard of:

> Hurry me, Nymphs, O, hurry me
> Far above the grovelling sea,
> Which, with blind weakness and bass roar
> Casting his white age on the shore,
> Wallows along that slimy floor;
> With his wide-spread webbèd hands
> Seeking to climb the level sands,
> But rejected still to rave
> Alive in his uncovered grave.

Admirers of the sea may call that a lampoon or a caricature, but they cannot deny that it is life-like: the man who wrote it had seen the sea, and the man who reads it sees the sea again.

Poor Swinburne! But Housman's criticism is terribly true. What he emphasizes and values is the ability of a poet to 'make you see': the talent, as it happens, that Joseph Conrad most valued in a novelist.

'The Larkin Automatic Car Wash'
by Gavin Ewart (1916–95)

An extremely versatile poet who worked in an advertising company, and was much admired as a 'poet's poet' by the poetical bohemians of his time. This poem is full of his understanding of and admiration for the way a Larkin poem works.

Back from the Palace of a famous king,
    Italian art
Making the roped-off rooms a Culture thing,
At about five o'clock we made a start,
Six teenagers squashed in. And as I drove
North from the barley sugar chimney pots
They sang the changeable teenager songs
That fade like tapestries those craftsmen wove,
But centuries more quickly. Through the knots
Of road-crossing pedestrians, through the longs

And shorts of planners' morse, the traffic lights,
    Over a hill,
Down to the garage advertising tights,
A special bargain, fast I drove on till
I drew up by the new Car Wash machine,
Pride of the forecourt, where a sign said STOP
Clear on the asphalt. In front a smaller car
Stood patiently as brushes swooshed it clean,
Whirling its streaming sides and back and top –
A travelling gantry; verticals, cross-bar.

We wound our windows up and waited there.
    In pixie green
The moving monster lifted itself clear,
The yellow brushes furled and now were seen
As plastic Christmas trees. Its wet last client

Made for the highway and it was our turn.
In gear and under. Two tenpences fed in
A slot on the driver's side. The pliant
Great brushes whirred and closed. Like yellow fern
One blurred the windscreen. Underwater thin

The Science Fiction light came creeping through
   Alien and weird
As when the vegetables invade in *Dr Who*,
Something to be amused at – almost feared.
And as the lateral brushes closed our sides,
Sweeping past steadily back, the illusion came
That *we* were moving forward; and I checked
The hard-on handbrake, thought of switchback rides
And how the effect in childhood was the same –
Momentary fear that gathered, to collect

In joy of safety. The tall half-children screamed –
   The girls at least –
Delighted to be frightened, as it seemed,
By this mechanical, otherworldly beast.
The boys made usual, window-opening, jokes.
And soon, tide-turning, the brushes travelled back,
Put our imaginations in reverse,
Though we were still. Like cigarettes and cokes
This was their slight excitement, took up slack
In time that wound by, idle. Nothing worse

And nothing better. To me it seemed so short,
   I wanted more,
I wanted hours, I wanted to be caught
In that dense undergrowth by that wet shore.
This was an exit from our boring life,
A changed environment, another place,
A hideout from the searchers. Otherness
Was that world's commonplace, a kitchen knife,
Something so usual that it had no face –
As the car dripped unnatural cleanliness.

Yes, it was jolly, *Fun for the kids* we say,
      But more than that;
For if you look at it another way
This was a notable peak where all is flat.
Into the main road by the riverside
We right-turned past the pubs that line the route
Where cheering crowds watch boat race crews go by,
Travelling with the full incoming tide.
The roof, the sides, the bonnet and the boot
Shone with new wetness. Yet the dust could lie

As thick there as before; and would, in time
      This was reprieve.
Cars too grow old and dirty. Gin-and-lime
Perks up the guest; but all guests have to leave.
In through the main gate of the block of flats
I drove my giggling adolescent load
And in vibrating door-slammed solitude
I parked. Under their different hats
Spiritual experiences work in a kind of code.
Did I have one? I, from this multitude?

'Absences'
by Philip Larkin
(1922–85)

'Absences' is my favourite among Larkin's poems. He was quite young when he wrote it, probably on his way to Ireland, to take up a position as a librarian at Queen's University, Belfast. All of which is only marginally relevant to the magic of the poem, just as Larkin's extremely negative views of life, politics, and society – you name it – are always in the background of his poetry. I feel that this negativism, as one would have to call it, is both bracing and comforting, as well as staying permanently in the mind in a uniquely and quietly haunting way. It has been pointed out that 'Absences' shows clearly that Larkin, who protested that he knew nothing about France or French poetry, had in fact been reading such abstruse French poets as Mallarmé.

Rain patters on a sea that tilts and sighs.
Fast-running floors, collapsing into hollows,
Tower suddenly, spray-haired. Contrariwise,
A wave drops like a wall: another follows,
Wilting and scrambling, tirelessly at play
Where there are no ships and no shallows.

Above the sea, the yet more shoreless day,
Riddled by wind, trails lit-up galleries:
They shift to giant ribbing, sift away.

Such attics cleared of me! Such absences!

'No Road'

'No Road' is about breaking off relations with a girlfriend or near fiancée, but it need not be anything so specific. It is confessional in its way, and again strangely comforting. The idea that one can break off relations with other human beings is obviously an attractive one at times. Who doesn't have longings for the pleasures of solitude and irresponsibility? Let others live if they want to, and enjoy life's pleasures. Larkin would rather be alone and try to write poems. He knows the drawbacks all too well, and this makes the lugubrious comic background of several of his poems.

Since we agreed to let the road between us
Fall to disuse,
And bricked our gates up, planted trees to screen us,
And turned all time's eroding agents loose,
Silence, and space, and strangers – our neglect
Has not had much effect.

Leaves drift unswept, perhaps; grass creeps unmown;
No other change.
So clear it stands, so little overgrown,
Walking that way tonight would not seem strange,
And still would be allowed. A little longer,
And time will be the stronger,

Drafting a world where no such road will run
From you to me;
To watch that world come up like a cold sun,
Rewarding others, is my liberty.
Not to prevent it is my will's fulfilment.
Willing it, my ailment.

'The Whitsun Weddings'

This is a good example of Larkin's attitude to relationships – perhaps indeed the most elaborate. The situation is so beautifully set up, just as it might be. The conclusion is that other people 'get under way' in life, but not the poet. And he prefers things that way because they give him the special life of his poems.

That Whitsun, I was late getting away:
    Not till about
One-twenty on the sunlit Saturday
Did my three-quarters-empty train pull out,
All windows down, all cushions hot, all sense
Of being in a hurry gone. We ran
Behind the backs of houses, crossed a street
Of blinding windscreens, smelt the fish-dock; thence
The river's level drifting breadth began,
Where sky and Lincolnshire and water meet.

All afternoon, through the tall heat that slept
    For miles inland,
A slow and stopping curve southwards we kept.
Wide farms went by, short-shadowed cattle, and
Canals with floatings of industrial froth;
A hothouse flashed uniquely: hedges dipped
And rose: and now and then a smell of grass
Displaced the reek of buttoned carriage-cloth
Until the next town, new and nondescript,
Approached with acres of dismantled cars.

At first, I didn't notice what a noise
    The weddings made
Each station that we stopped at: sun destroys
The interest of what's happening in the shade,
And down the long cool platforms whoops and skirls
I took for porters larking with the mails,

And went on reading. Once we started, though,
We passed them, grinning and pomaded, girls
In parodies of fashion, heels and veils,
All posed irresolutely, watching us go,

As if out on the end of an event
   Waving goodbye
To something that survived it. Struck, I leant
More promptly out next time, more curiously,
And saw it all again in different terms:
The fathers with broad belts under their suits
And seamy foreheads; mothers loud and fat;
An uncle shouting smut; and then the perms,
The nylon gloves and jewellery-substitutes,
The lemons, mauves, and olive-ochres that

Marked off the girls unreally from the rest.
   Yes, from cafés
And banquet-halls up yards, and bunting-dressed
Coach-party annexes, the wedding-days
Were coming to an end. All down the line
Fresh couples climbed aboard: the rest stood round;
The last confetti and advice were thrown,
And, as we moved, each face seemed to define
Just what it saw departing: children frowned
At something dull; fathers had never known

Success so huge and wholly farcical;
   The women shared
The secret like a happy funeral;
While girls, gripping their handbags tighter, stared
At a religious wounding. Free at last,
And loaded with the sum of all they saw,
We hurried towards London, shuffling gouts of steam.
Now fields were building-plots, and poplars cast
Long shadows over major roads, and for
Some fifty minutes, that in time would seem

Just long enough to settle hats and say
  I nearly died,
A dozen marriages got under way.
They watched the landscape, sitting side by side
– An Odeon went past, a cooling tower,
And someone running up to bowl – and none
Thought of the others they would never meet
Or how their lives would all contain this hour.
I thought of London spread out in the sun,
Its postal districts packed like squares of wheat:

There we were aimed. And as we raced across
  Bright knots of rail
Past standing Pullmans, walls of blackened moss
Came close, and it was nearly done, this frail
Travelling coincidence; and what it held
Stood ready to be loosed with all the power
That being changed can give. We slowed again,
And as the tightened brakes took hold, there swelled
A sense of falling, like an arrow-shower
Sent out of sight, somewhere becoming rain.

'Trapping Fairies'
by Gelett Burgess
(1866–1931)

I don't know why I find this little poem so enchanting, perhaps because West Virginia seems essentially a comic place with lots of trouble and nothing much to eat. The fairies suffer as much as the human beings. Was that why the poet was reduced to trapping them?

The author (who was he, I wonder, and what did he do?) also wrote the famous verse about the Purple Cow, which may have once had amusement value, but has it no longer.

Again for no reason, I associate 'Trapping Fairies' with 'A Fine Romance' by Dorothy Fields (1904–74), which follows. Iris used sometimes to sing it with great brio.

Trapping fairies in West Virginia:
I think I never saw fairies skinnier.

'A Fine Romance'
by Dorothy Fields
(1904–74)

She   A fine romance! with no kisses!
A fine romance, my friend, this is!
We should be like a couple of hot tomatoes,
But you're as cold as yesterday's mashed potatoes.
A fine romance! you won't nestle,
A fine romance, you won't wrestle!
I might as well play bridge with my maiden aunts!
I haven't got a chance.
This is a fine romance!

A fine romance! my good fellow!
You take romance, I'll take Jello!
You're calmer than the seals in the Arctic Ocean,
At least they flap their fins to express emotion.
A fine romance! with no quarrels,
With no insults, and all morals!
I've never mussed the crease in your blue serge pants,
I never get the chance.
This is a fine romance!

He A fine romance! with no kisses!
A fine romance, my friend, this is!

We two should be like clams in a dish of chowder,
But we just fizz like parts of a Seidlitz powder.
A fine romance, with no clinches,
A fine romance, with no pinches,
You're just as hard to land as the 'Île de France'!
I haven't got a chance.
This is a fine romance!

A fine romance! my dear Duchess!
Two old fogies who need crutches!
True love should have the thrills that a healthy
            crime has!
We don't have half the thrill that the 'March of Time'
            has!
A fine romance, my good woman!
My strong 'Aged in the Wood' woman!
You never give the orchids I sent a glance!
No! you like cactus plants.
This is a fine romance!

'The Cod'

by T. E. Brown

(1830–97)

Brown is still notorious today for one short poem – 'A Garden is a Lovesome Thing, God Wot!' These poems show that he could do much better. The codfish certainly sticks in my mind, as does the Englishwoman on the Pincian Hill. Brown had a sense of humour which does not seem in the least Victorian.

High overhead
   My little daughter
Was going to bed: –
   Below
   In twenty fathoms of black water
   A cod went sulking slow –
Perceived the light
That sparkled on the height,
   Then swam
Up to the filmy level,
   Brought's eye to bear
   With dull fixed stare,
   Then – 'Damn!'
He said – and 'Devil! –
I thought' – but what he thought who knows?
One plunge, and off he goes
   East? North?
   Fares forth
To Lundy? Cardiff? But of that keen probe
That for an instant pierced the lobe

   Of his sad brain,
Tickling the phosphor-grit,
   How long will he retain
One bit?

And then above
My little daughter kneels, and says her prayers.
    Quite right!
        My little love –
Good night!
        Sweet pet!
Put out the light!
        And so
            I go
Downstairs –
And yet – and yet –
        That cod!
        O God!
        O God!

From *Roman Women*

XIII

O Englishwoman on the Pincian,
I love you not, nor ever can –
Astounding woman on the Pincian!

I know your mechanism well-adjusted,
I see your mind and body have been trusted
To all the proper people:
I see you straight as is a steeple;
I see you are not old;
I see you are a rich man's daughter;
I see you know the use of gold,
But also know the use of soap-and-water;
And yet I love you not, nor ever can –
Distinguished woman on the Pincian!

You have no doubt of your preëminence,
Nor do I make pretence
To challenge it for my poor little slattern,
Whose costume dates from Saturn –
My wall-flower with the long, love-draggled fringes:
But then the controversy hinges
On higher forms; and you must bear
Comparisons more noble. Stare, yes, stare –
I love you not, nor ever can,
You peerless woman on the Pincian.

No, you'll not see her on the Pincian,
My Roman woman, wife of Roman man!
Elsewhere you may –
And she is bright as is the day;
And she is sweet, that honest workman's wife
Fulfilled with bounteous life:
Her body balanced like a spring
In equipoise of perfect natural grace;
Her soul unquestioning
Of ought but genial cares; her face,
Her frock, her attitude, her pace
The confluence of absolute harmonies –
And you, my Lady Margaret,
Pray what have you to set
'Gainst splendours such as these?
No, I don't love you, and I never can
Pretentious woman on the Pincian!

But morals – beautiful serenity
Of social life, the sugar and the tea
The flannels and the soup, the coals,
The patent recipes for saving souls,
And other things: the chill dead sneer
Conventional, the abject fear
Of form-transgressing freedom – I admit
That you have these; but love you not a whit

The more, nor ever can,
Alarming female on the Pincian!

Come out, O woman, from this blindness!
Rome, too, has women full of loving-kindness
Has noble women, perfect in all good
That makes the glory of great womanhood –
But they are Women! I have seen them bent
On gracious errand; seen how goodness lent
The grave, ineffable charm
That guards from possibility of harm
A creature so divinely made,
So softly swayed
With native gesture free –
The melting-point of passionate purity.
Yes – soup and flannels too,
And tickets for them – just like you –
Tracts, books, and all the innumerable channels
Through which your bounty acts –
Well – not the tracts,

But certainly the flannels –
Her I must love, but you I never can,
Unlovely woman on the Pincian.

And yet –
Remarkable woman on the Pincian! –
We owe a sort of debt
To you, as having gone with us of old
To those bleak islands, cold
And desolate and grim,
Upon the Ocean's rim,
And shared their horrors with us – not that then
Our poor bewildered ken
Could catch the further issues, knowing only
That we were very lonely!
Ah well, you did us service in your station;

And how the progress of our civilisation
Has made you quite so terrible
It boots not ask; for still
You gave us stalwart scions,
Suckled the young sea-lions,
And smiled infrequent, glacial smiles
Upon the sulky isles –
For this and all His mercies – stay at home!
Here are the passion-flowers!
Here are the sunny hours!
O Pincian woman, do not come to Rome!

From *A Tale of Two Cities* (1859)
by Charles Dickens
(1812–70)

In this masterly passage, Dickens shows what an imaginative historian lurked somewhere within him. He often reminds us sharply in his fiction how perfectly abominable history was, and how often even sensible people tend to sentimentalize it.

It was the year of Our Lord one thousand seven hundred and seventy-five. Spiritual revelations were conceded to England at that favoured period, as at this. Mrs. Southcott had recently attained her five-and-twentieth blessed birthday, of whom a prophetic private in the Life Guards had heralded the sublime appearance by announcing that arrangements were made for the swallowing up of London and Westminster. Even the Cock-lane ghost had been laid only a round dozen of years, after rapping out its messages, as the spirits of this very year last past (supernaturally deficient in originality) rapped out theirs. Mere messages in the earthly order of events had lately come to the English Crown and People, from a congress of British subjects in America: which, strange to relate, have proved more important to the human race than any communications yet received through any of the chickens of the Cock-lane brood.

France, less favoured on the whole as to matters spiritual than her sister of the shield and trident, rolled with exceeding smoothness down hill, making paper money and spending it. Under the guidance of her Christian pastors, she entertained herself, besides, with such humane achievements as sentencing a youth to have his hands cut off, his tongue torn out with pincers, and his body burned alive, because he had not kneeled down in the rain to do honour to a dirty procession of monks which passed within his view, at a distance of some fifty or sixty yards. It is likely enough that, rooted in the woods of France and Norway, there were growing trees, when that sufferer was put to death, already marked by the Wooodman, Fate, to come down and be sawn into boards, to make a certain movable framework with a sack and a knife in it, terrible in history. It is likely enough that in the rough outhouses of some tillers of the heavy lands adjacent to Paris, there were sheltered from the weather that very day, rude carts, bespattered with rustic mire, snuffed about by pigs, and roosted in by poultry, which the Farmer, Death, had already set apart to be his tumbrils of the Revolution. But that Woodman and that Farmer, though they work unceasingly, work silently, and no one heard them as they went about with muffled tread: the rather, forasmuch as to entertain any suspicion that they were awake, was to be atheistical and traitorous.

In England, there was scarcely an amount of order and protection to justify much national boasting. Daring burglaries by armed men, and highway robberies, took place in the capital itself every night; families were publicly cautioned not to go out of town without removing their furniture to upholsterers' warehouses for security; the highwayman in the dark was a City tradesman in the light, and, being recognised and challenged by his fellow-tradesman whom he stopped in his character of 'the Captain,' gallantly shot him through the head and rode away; the mail was waylaid by seven robbers, and the guard shot three dead, and then got shot dead himself by the other four, 'in consequence of the failure of his ammunition:' after which the mail was robbed in peace; that magnificent potentate, the Lord Mayor of London, was made to stand and deliver on Turnham Green, by one highwayman, who despoiled the illustrious creature in sight of all his retinue; prisoners in London gaols fought battles with their turnkeys, and the majesty of the law fired blunderbusses in among them, loaded with rounds of shot and ball; thieves snipped off diamond crosses from the necks of noble lords at Court drawing-rooms; musketeers went into St. Giles's, to search for contraband goods, and the mob fired on the musketeers, and the musketeers fired on the mob, and nobody thought any of these occurrences much out of the common way. In the midst of them, the hangman, ever busy and ever worse than useless, was in constant requisition; now, stringing up long rows of miscellaneous criminals; now, hanging a housebreaker on Saturday who had been taken on Tuesday; now, burning people in the hand at Newgate by the dozen, and now burning pamphlets at the door of Westminster Hall; to-day, taking the life of an atrocious murderer, and to-morrow of a wretched pilferer who had robbed a farmer's boy of sixpence.

All these things, and a thousand like them, came to pass in and close upon the dear old year one thousand seven hundred and seventy-five. Environed by them, while the Woodman and the Farmer worked unheeded, those two of the large jaws, and those other two of the plain and the fair faces, trod with stir enough, and carried their divine rights with a high hand. Thus did the year one thousand seven hundred and seventy-five conduct their Greatnesses, and myriads of small creatures – the creatures of this chronicle among the rest – along the roads that lay before them.

'Lot's Wife'

by Anna Akhmatova

(1889–1966)

These two wonderful poetic perceptions of the story of Lot and its human implications have something else in common. Both of them come off brilliantly in terms of poems that realize completely a sudden intuition of the poet.

And the just man trailed God's shining agent,
over a black mountain, in his giant track,
while a restless voice kept harrying his woman:
'It's not too late, you can still look back

at the red towers of your native Sodom,
the square where once you sang, the spinning-shed,
at the empty windows set in the tall house
where sons and daughters blessed your marriage-bed.'

A single glance: a sudden dart of pain
stitching her eyes before she made a sound . . .
Her body flaked into transparent salt,
and her swift legs rooted to the ground.

Who will grieve for this woman? Does she not seem
too insignificant for our concern?
Yet in my heart I never will deny her,
who suffered death because she chose to turn.

'Number XXXV' from *More Poems*
by A. E. Housman
(1859–1936)

Half-way, for one commandment broken.
    The woman made her endless halt.
And she to-day, a glistering token,
    Stands in the wilderness of salt.
Behind, the vats of judgement brewing
    Thundered, and thick the brimstone snowed;
He to the hill of his undoing
    Pursued his road.

'The Scholar-Gipsy'
by Matthew Arnold
(1822–88)

*Matthew Arnold was fascinated by this character who existed histori-
cally and roamed around Oxford in much the way that Arnold
describes. Perhaps all scholars, administrators, and worldly people –
and Arnold was all three – have a secret hankering to give it all up and
lead the free life of a scholar-gipsy. Certainly it is this, not-so-deeply-
hidden desire which gives the poem its plangency and conveys
something to which, as Dr Johnson said of Gray's 'Elegy', 'Every
bosom returns an echo'.*

Go, for they call you, shepherd, from the hill;
   Go, shepherd, and untie the wattled cotes!
      No longer leave thy wistful flock unfed,
   Nor let thy bawling fellows rack their throats,
   Nor the cropped herbage shoot another head.
      But when the fields are still,
And the tired men and dogs all gone to rest,
   And only the white sheep are sometimes seen
   Cross and recross the strips of moon-blanched green,
Come, shepherd, and again begin the quest!

Here, where the reaper was at work of late –
   In this high field's dark corner, where he leaves
      His coat, his basket, and his earthen cruse,
   And in the sun all morning binds the sheaves,
      Then here, at noon, comes back his stores to use –
      Here will I sit and wait,
   While to my ear from uplands far away
      The bleating of the folded flocks is borne,
      With distant cries of reapers in the corn –
   All the live murmur of a summer's day.
Screened is this nook o'er the high, half-reaped field,

And here till sun-down, shepherd! will I be.
Through the thick corn the scarlet poppies peep,
And round green roots and yellowing stalks I see
Pale pink convolvulus in tendrils creep;
And air-swept lindens yield
Their scent, and rustle down their perfumed showers
Of bloom on the bent grass where I am laid,
And bower me from the August sun with shade;
And the eye travels down to Oxford's towers.

And near me on the grass lies Glanvil's book –
Come, let me read the oft-read tale again!
The story of the Oxford scholar poor,
Of pregnant parts and quick inventive brain,
Who, tired of knocking at preferment's door,
One summer-morn forsook
His friends, and went to learn the gipsy-lore,
And roamed the world with that wild brotherhood,
And came, as most men deemed, to little good,
But came to Oxford and his friends no more.

But once, years after, in the country-lanes,
Two scholars, whom at college erst he knew,
Met him, and of his way of life enquired;
Whereat he answered, that the gipsy-crew,
His mates, had arts to rule as they desired
The workings of men's brains,
And they can bind them to what thoughts they will.
'And I,' he said, 'the secret of their art,
When fully learned, will to the world impart;
But it needs heaven-sent moments for this skill.'

This said, he left them, and returned no more.
But rumours hung about the country-side,
That the lost Scholar long was seen to stray,
Seen by rare glimpses, pensive and tongue-tied,
In hat of antique shape, and cloak of grey,

The same the gipsies wore.
Shepherds had met him on the Hurst in spring;
    At some lone alehouse in the Berkshire moors,
    On the warm ingle-bench, the smock-frocked
        boors
Had found him seated at their entering,

But, 'mid their drink and clatter, he would fly.
    And I myself seem half to know thy looks,
        And put the shepherds, wanderer! on thy trace;
    And boys who in lone wheatfields scare the rooks
        I ask if thou hast passed their quiet place;
            Or in my boat I lie
    Moored to the cool bank in the summer-heats,
        'Mid wide grass meadows which the sunshine fills,
        And watch the warm, green-muffled Cumner hills,
    And wonder if thou haunt'st their shy retreats.

For most, I know, thou lov'st retiréd ground!
    Thee at the ferry Oxford riders blithe,
        Returning home on summer-nights, have met
    Crossing the stripling Thames at Bab-lock-hithe,
        Trailing in the cool stream thy fingers wet,
            As the punt's rope chops round;
    And leaning backward in a pensive dream,
        And fostering in thy lap a heap of flowers
        Plucked in shy fields and distant Wychwood
            bowers,
    And thine eyes resting on the moonlit stream.

And then they land, and thou art seen no more!
    Maidens, who from the distant hamlets come
        To dance around the Fyfield elm in May,
    Oft through the darkening fields have seen thee
        roam,
        Or cross a stile into the public way.
            Oft thou hast given them store

Of flowers – the frail-leafed, white anemone,
　　Dark bluebells drenched with dews of summer eves,
　　And purple orchises with spotted leaves –
But none hath words she can report of thee.

And, above Godstow Bridge, when hay-time's here
　　In June, and many a scythe in sunshine flames,
　　　Men who through those wide fields of breezy grass
　Where black-winged swallows haunt the glittering
　　　To bathe in the abandoned lasher pass, [Thames,
　　　　Have often passed thee near
　Sitting upon the river bank o'ergrown;
　　Marked thine outlandish garb, thy figure spare,
　　Thy dark vague eyes, and soft abstracted air –
But, when they came from bathing, thou wast gone!

At some lone homestead in the Cumner hills,
　　Where at her open door the housewife darns,
　　　Thou hast been seen, or hanging on a gate
　To watch the threshers in the mossy barns.
　　　Children, who early range these slopes and late
　　　　For cresses from the rills,
　Have known thee eying, all an April-day,
　　The springing pastures and the feeding kine;
　　And marked thee, when the stars come out and shine,
Through the long dewy grass move slow away.

In autumn, on the skirts of Bagley Wood –
　　Where most the gipsies by the turf-edged way
　　　Pitch their smoked tents, and every bush you see
　With scarlet patches tagged and shreds of grey,
　　　Above the forest-ground called Thessaly –
　　　　The blackbird, picking food,
　Sees thee, nor stops his meal, nor fears at all;
　　So often has he known thee past him stray,
　　Rapt, twirling in thy hand a withered spray,
And waiting for the spark from heaven to fall.

And once, in winter, on the causeway chill
　　Where home through flooded fields foot-travellers go,
　　　Have I not passed thee on the wooden bridge,
　　Wrapped in thy cloak and battling with the snow,
　　　Thy face tow'rd Hinksey and its wintry ridge?
　　　　And thou hast climbed the hill,
　　And gained the white brow of the Cumner range;
　　　Turned once to watch, while thick the snowflakes
　　　The line of festal light in Christ-Church hall – [fall,
　　Then sought thy straw in some sequestered grange.

But what – I dream! Two hundred years are flown
　　Since first thy story ran through Oxford halls,
　　　And the grave Glanvil did the tale inscribe
　　That thou wert wandered from the studious walls
　　　To learn strange arts, and join a gipsy-tribe;
　　　　And thou from earth art gone
　　Long since, and in some quiet churchyard laid –
　　　Some country-nook, where o'er thy unknown
　　　　　grave
　　　Tall grasses and white flowering nettles wave,
　　Under a dark, red-fruited yew-tree's shade.

No, no, thou hast not felt the lapse of hours!
　　For what wears out the life of mortal men?
　　　'Tis that from change to change their being rolls;
　　'Tis that repeated shocks, again, again,
　　　Exhaust the energy of strongest souls
　　　　And numb the elastic powers.
　　Till having used our nerves with bliss and teen,
　　　And tired upon a thousand schemes our wit,
　　　To the just-pausing Genius we remit
　　Our worn-out life, and are – what we have been.
　　Thou hast not lived, why should'st thou perish, so?
　　　Thou hadst *one* aim, *one* business, *one* desire;
　　　　Else wert thou long since numbered with the dead!
　　Else hadst thou spent, like other men, thy fire!

The generations of thy peers are fled,
And we ourselves shall go;
But thou possessest an immortal lot,
And we imagine thee exempt from age
And living as thou liv'st on Glanvil's page,
Because thou hadst – what we, alas! have not.

For early didst thou leave the world, with powers
Fresh, undiverted to the world without,
Firm to their mark, not spent on other things;
Free from the sick fatigue, the languid doubt,
Which much to have tried, in much been baffled,
brings.
O life unlike to ours !
Who fluctuate idly without term or scope,
Of whom each strives, nor knows for what he strives,
And each half-lives a hundred different lives;
Who wait like thee, but not, like thee, in hope.

Thou waitest for the spark from heaven! and we,
Light half-believers of our casual creeds,
Who never deeply felt, nor clearly willed,
Whose insight never has borne fruit in deeds,
Whose vague resolves never have been fulfilled;
For whom each year we see
Breeds new beginnings, disappointments new;
Who hesitate and falter life away,
And lose to-morrow the ground won to-day –
Ah! do not we, wanderer! await it too?

Yes, we await it! – but it still delays,
And then we suffer! and amongst us one,
Who most has suffered, takes dejectedly
His seat upon the intellectual throne;
And all his store of sad experience he
Lays bare of wretched days;
Tells us his misery's birth and growth and signs,

And how the dying spark of hope was fed,
    And how the breast was soothed, and how the head,
And all his hourly varied anodynes.

This for our wisest! and we others pine,
    And wish the long unhappy dream would end,
        And waive all claim to bliss, and try to bear;
    With close-lipped patience for our only friend,
        Sad patience, too near neighbour to despair –
            But none has hope like thine!
    Thou through the fields and through the woods
                dost stray,
        Roaming the country-side, a truant boy,
        Nursing thy project in unclouded joy,
    And every doubt long blown by time away.

O born in days when wits were fresh and clear,
    And life ran gaily as the sparkling Thames;
        Before this strange disease of modern life,
    With its sick hurry, its divided aims,
        Its heads o'ertaxed, its palsied hearts, was rife –
            Fly hence, our contact fear!
    Still fly, plunge deeper in the bowering wood!
        Averse, as Dido did with gesture stern
        From her false friend's approach in Hades turn,
    Wave us away, and keep thy solitude!

Still nursing the unconquerable hope,
    Still clutching the inviolable shade,
        With a free, onward impulse brushing through,
    By night, the silvered branches of the glade –
        Far on the forest-skirts, where none pursue,
            On some mild pastoral slope
    Emerge, and resting on the moonlit pales
        Freshen thy flowers as in former years
            With dew, or listen with enchanted ears,
    From the dark dingles, to the nightingales!

But fly our paths, our feverish contact fly!
  For strong the infection of our mental strife,
      Which, though it gives no bliss, yet spoils for
          rest;
And we should win thee from thy own fair life,
  Like us distracted, and like us unblest.
          Soon, soon thy cheer would die,
Thy hopes grow timorous, and unfixed thy powers,
  And thy clear aims be cross and shifting made;
  And then thy glad perennial youth would fade,
Fade, and grow old at last, and die like ours.

'Lovely Pamela'
by Richard Usborne
(1910–   )

A touching little epigram by an author who happened to write the definitive, and wonderfully readable, survey of those popular heroes and villains of the 1920s and 1930s: Richard Hannay, Bulldog Drummond, Dr Fu Man-chu.

Lovely Pamela, who found
One sure way to get around
Goes to bed beneath this stone
Early, sober, and alone.

From *Under the Net* (1954)
by Iris Murdoch
(1919–99)

Iris Murdoch's first novel has many delights. This commentary on philosophy, and the teaching of it, was very much one of them.

There are some parts of London which are necessary and others which are contingent. Everywhere west of Earls Court is contingent, except for a few places along the river. I hate contingency. I want everything in my life to have a sufficient reason. Dave lived west of Earls Court, and this was another thing I had against him. He lived off the Goldhawk Road, in one of those reddish black buildings which for some reason are called mansions. It was in such contexts, in my dark London childhood, that I first learnt the word, and it has ruined many pieces of prose for me since, including some Biblical ones. I think that Dave doesn't mind much about his surroundings. Being a philosopher, he is professionally concerned with the central knot of being (though he would hate to hear me use this phrase), and not with the loose ends that most of us have to play with. Also, since he is Jewish he can feel himself to be a part of History without making any special effort. I envy him that. For myself, I find I have to work harder and harder every year to keep in with History. So Dave can afford to have a contingent address. I wasn't sure that I could.

Dave's mansions are tall, but they are overhung by a huge modern hospital, with white walls, which stands next to them. A place of simplicity and justification, which I pass with a *frisson*. Now as I came up the dark stained-glass staircase to Dave's flat I heard a hum of voices. This displeased me. Dave knows far too many people. His life is a continual *tour de force* of intimacy. I myself would think it immoral to be intimate with more than four people at any given time. But Dave seems to be on intimate terms with more than a hundred. He has a large and clinging acquaintance among artists and intellectuals, and he knows many leftwing political people too, including oddities such as Lefty Todd, the leader of the New Independent Socialist Party, and others of even greater eccentricity. Then there are his pupils, and the friends of his pupils, and the ever-growing horde of his ex-pupils. No one whom Dave has taught seems ever to lose touch with him. I find this, in a way, hard to understand, since as I have indicated Dave was never able to communicate anything to me when we talked about philosophy. But perhaps I am too much the incorrigible artist, as he once exclaimed. This reminds me to add that Dave disapproves of the way I live, and is always urging me to take a regular job.

Dave does extra-mural work for the University, and collects about him many youths who have a part-time interest in truth. Dave's pupils adore him, but there is a permanent fight on between him and them. They aspire like sunflowers. They are all natural metaphysicians, or so Dave says in a tone of disgust. This seems to me a wonderful thing to be, but it inspires in Dave a passion of opposition. To Dave's pupils the world is a mystery; a mystery to which it should be reasonably possible to discover a key. The key would be something of the sort that could be contained in a book of some eight hundred pages. To find the key would not necessarily be a simple matter, but Dave's pupils feel sure that the dedication of between four and ten hours a week, excluding University vacations, should suffice to find it. They do not conceive that the matter should be either more simple or more complex than that. They are prepared within certain limits to alter their views. Many of them arrive as theosophists and depart as Critical Realists or Bradleians. It is remarkable how Dave's criticism seems so often to be purely catalytic in its action. He blazes upon them with the destructive fury of the sun, but instead of shrivelling up their metaphysical pretensions, achieves merely their metamorphosis from one rich stage into another. This curious fact makes me think that perhaps after all Dave is, in spite of himself, a good teacher. Occasionally he succeeds in converting some peculiarly receptive youth to his own brand of linguistic analysis; after which as often as not the youth loses interest in philosophy altogether. To watch Dave at work on these young men is like watching someone prune a rose bush. It is all the strongest and most luxuriant shoots which have to come off. Then later perhaps there will be blossoms; but not philosophical ones, Dave trusts. His great aim is to dissuade the young from philosophy. He always warns me off it with particular earnestness.

'Somewhere or Other'
by Christina Rossetti
(1830–94)

As a poet Christina Rossetti is highly accomplished, as accomplished as Tennyson, and her best poems seem to speak to us more directly than he does, always intimately and without pretension. How many people leading lonely or secluded lives must have felt exactly as she does?

Somewhere or other there must surely be
    The face not seen, the voice not heard,
The heart that not yet – never yet – ah me!
    Made answer to my word.

Somewhere or other, may be near or far;
    Past land and sea, clean out of sight;
Beyond the wandering moon, beyond the star
    That tracks her night by night.

Somewhere or other, may be far or near;
    With just a wall, a hedge, between;
With just the last leaves of the dying year
    Fallen on a turf grown green.

'Poor Honest Men (A.D. 1800)'
by Rudyard Kipling
(1865–1936)

Smugglers are romantic figures, but Kipling is much more interested in how they actually go about it – from the tobacco field in Virginia to the parson's pipe in the English shires. He probably did not exaggerate the hazards of the trade, and his eye for technical detail is always masterly. (A ship whose foresails are damaged by gunfire could not maintain a course in pursuit, so the smugglers try to disable the revenue ship by this method.)

Your jar of Virginny
Will cost you a guinea,
Which you reckon too much by five shillings or ten;
But light your churchwarden
And judge it according,
When I've told you the troubles of poor honest men.

From the Capes of the Delaware,
As you are well aware,
We sail with tobacco for England – but then,
Our own British cruisers,
They watch us come through, sirs,
And they press half a score of us poor honest men!

Or if by quick sailing
(Thick weather prevailing)
We leave them behind (as we do now and then)
We are sure of a gun from
Each frigate we run from,
Which is often destruction to poor honest men!

Broadsides the Atlantic
We tumble short-handed,

With shot-holes to plug and new canvas to bend;
And off the Azores,
Dutch, Dons and Monsieurs
Are waiting to terrify poor honest men.

Napoleon's embargo
Is laid on all cargo
Which comfort or aid to King George may intend;
And since roll, twist and leaf,
Of all comforts is chief,
They try for to steal it from poor honest men!

With no heart for fight,
We take refuge in flight
But fire as we run, our retreat to defend;
Until our stern-chasers
Cut up her fore-braces,
And she flies off the wind from us poor honest men!

'Twix' the Forties and Fifties,
South-eastward the drift is,
And so, when we think we are making Land's End,
Alas, it is Ushant
With half the King's Navy,
Blockading French ports against poor honest men!

But they may not quit station
(Which is our salvation)
So swiftly we stand to the Nor'ard again;
And finding the tail of
A homeward-bound convoy,
We slip past the Scillies like poor honest men.

'Twix' the Lizard and Dover,
We hand our stuff over,
Though I may not inform how we do it, nor when.
But a light on each quarter,

Low down on the water,
Is well understanded by poor honest men.

Even then we have dangers,
From meddlesome strangers,
Who spy on our business and are not content
To take a smooth answer,
Except with a handspike . . .
And they say they are murdered by poor honest men!

To be drowned or be shot
Is our natural lot,
Why should we, moreover, be hanged in the end –
After all our great pains
For to dangle in chains
As though we were smugglers, not poor honest men?

'After'

by Rudyard Kipling
(1865–1936)

Kipling's poems on the American Revolution are much less well-known, but they are some of his best. His journalistic eye and ear were brilliant, and he gives us a quick insight into the eighteenth-century situation in America, with the English fighting to protect their colonists from a French takeover, and being evicted in their turn by the newly secure and self-confident American states.

The snow lies thick on Valley Forge,
    The ice on the Delaware,
But the poor dead soldiers of King George
    They neither know nor care.

Not though the earliest primrose break
    On the sunny side of the lane,
And scuffling rookeries awake
    Their England's spring again.

They will not stir when the drifts are gone,
    Or the ice melts out of the bay:
And the men that served with Washington
    Lie all as still as they.

They will not stir though the mayflower blows
    In the moist dark woods of pine,
And every rock-strewn pasture shows
    Mullein and columbine.

Each for his land, in a fair fight,
    Encountered, strove, and died,
And the kindly earth that knows no spite
    Covers them side by side.

She is too busy to think of war;
  She has all the world to make gay;
And, behold, the yearly flowers are
  Where they were in our fathers' day!

Golden-rod by the pasture-wall
  When the columbine is dead,
And sumach leaves that turn, in fall,
  Bright as the blood they shed.

'The Rainy Summer'
by Alice Meynell
(1847–1922)

For some reason I associate these two poems in my mind, perhaps because both have a kind of lilting musical memorability which is full of delicious melancholy. The poets themselves were very different. Flecker's little poem shows nostalgia for the rough life, and being dans le vrai, *which was not untypical of poets and intellectuals in the 1890s.*

There's much afoot in heaven and earth this year;
    The winds hunt up the sun, hunt up the moon,
Trouble the dubious dawn, hasten the drear
    Height of a threatening noon.

No breath of boughs, no breath of leaves, of fronds,
    May linger or grow warm; the trees are loud;
The forest, rooted, tosses in her bonds,
    And strains against the cloud.

No scents may pause within the garden-fold;
    The rifled flowers are cold as ocean-shells;
Bees, humming in the storm, carry their cold
    Wild honey to cold cells.

'Rioupéroux'
by J. E. Flecker
(1884–1915)

High and solemn mountains guard Rioupéroux
– Small untidy village where the river drives a mill –
Frail as wood anemones, white and frail were you,
And drooping a little, like the slender daffodil.

O I will go to France again, and tramp the valley through,
And I will change these gentle clothes for clog and corduroy,
And work with the mill-hands of black Rioupéroux,
And walk with you, and talk with you, like any other boy.

'The Eve of St Agnes'
by John Keats
(1795–1821)

There was a time when the Cambridge School of Criticism dismissed 'The Eve of St Agnes' as an example of Keats at his most cloying and mawkish. This was not the view of critics of Keats' own time, nor of the common reader since. The magical atmosphere of the poem is extraordinarily detailed – it was a favourite among the Pre-Raphaelites – but it also contains dark inklings of threat and danger, summed up in Keats' image of the tiger moth ('As are the tiger moth's deep damask wings'). Chill and warmth, soft luxury and mysterious terror go together in the poem and are fused into a dream-like whole. Inspiration came from the romances of Mrs Radcliffe, highly popular at the time.

The 'Ode on Indolence' is probably a poem about drugs, but it contrives again to use detail in a true Keatsian manner, humorously and with a kind of solemn pleasure in portraying the detail on the Urn, and the moist May morning.

I

St. Agnes' Eve – Ah, bitter chill it was!
The owl, for all his feathers, was a-cold;
The hare lump'd trembling through the frozen grass,
And silent was the flock in woolly fold:
Numb were the Beadsman's fingers, while he told
His rosary, and while his frosted breath,
Like pious incense from a censer old,
Seem'd taking flight for heaven, without a death,
Past the sweet Virgin's picture, while his prayer he saith.

II

His prayer he saith, this patient, holy man;
Then takes his lamp, and riseth from his knees,
And back returneth, meagre, barefoot, wan,
Along the chapel aisle by slow degrees:
The sculptur'd dead, on each side, seem to freeze,

Emprison'd in black, purgatorial rails:
Knights, ladies, praying in dumb orat'ries,
He passeth by; and his weak spirit fails
To think how they may ache in icy hoods and mails.

III

Northward he turneth through a little door,
And scarce three steps, ere Music's golden tongue
Flatter'd to tears this aged man and poor;
But no – already had his deathbell rung;
The joys of all his life were said and sung:
His was harsh penance on St. Agnes' Eve:
Another way he went, and soon among
Rough ashes sat he for his soul's reprieve,
And all night kept awake, for sinners' sake to grieve.

IV

That ancient Beadsman heard the prelude soft;
And so it chanc'd, for many a door was wide,
From hurry to and fro. Soon, up aloft,
The silver, snarling trumpets 'gan to chide:
The level chambers, ready with their pride,
Were glowing to receive a thousand guests:
The carved angels, ever eager-eyed,
Star'd, where upon their heads the cornice rests,
With hair blown back, and wings put cross-wise on their breasts.

V

At length burst in the argent revelry,
With plume, tiara, and all rich array,
Numerous as shadows haunting fairily
The brain, new-stuff'd, in youth, with triumphs gay
Of old romance. These let us wish away,
And turn, sole-thoughted, to one Lady there,
Whose heart had brooded, all that wintry day,
On love, and wing'd St. Agnes' saintly care,
As she had heard old dames full many times declare.

VI

They told her how, upon St. Agnes' Eve,
Young virgins might have visions of delight
And soft adorings from their loves receive
Upon the honey'd middle of the night,
If ceremonies due they did aright;
As, supperless to bed they must retire,
And couch supine their beauties, lily white;
Nor look behind, nor sideways, but require
Of Heaven with upward eyes for all that they desire.

VII

Full of this whim was thoughtful Madeline:
The music, yearning like a God in pain
She scarcely heard: her maiden eyes divine,
Fix'd on the floor, saw many a sweeping train
Pass by – she heeded not at all: in vain
Came many a tiptoe, amorous cavalier,
And back retir'd; not cool'd by high disdain,
Bnt she saw not: her heart was otherwhere:
She sigh'd for Agnes' dreams, the sweetest of the year.

VIII

She danc'd along with vague, regardless eyes,
Anxious her lips, her breathing quick and short:
The hallow'd hour was near at hand: she sighs
Amid the timbrels, and the throng'd resort
Of whisperers in anger, or in sport;
'Mid looks of love, defiance, hate, and scorn
Hoodwink'd with faery fancy; all amort
Save to St. Agnes and her lambs unshorn,
And all the bliss to be before to-morrow morn.

IX

So, purposing each moment to retire,
She linger'd still. Meantime, across the moors,
Had come young Porphyro, with heart on fire

For Madeline. Beside the portal doors,
Buttress'd from moonlight, stands he, and implores
All saints to give him sight of Madeline,
But for one moment in the tedious hours,
That he might gaze and worship all unseen;
Perchance speak, kneel, touch, kiss – in sooth such things
have been.

X

He ventures in: let no buzz'd whisper tell:
All eyes be muffled, or a hundred swords
Will storm his heart, Love's fev'rous citadel:
For him, those chambers held barbarian hordes,
Hyena foemen, and hot-blooded lords,
Whose very dogs would execrations howl
Against his lineage: not one breast affords
Him any mercy, in that mansion foul,
Save one old beldame, weak in body and in soul.

XI

Ah, happy chance! the aged creature came,
Shuffling along with ivory-headed wand,
To where he stood, hid from the torch's flame,
Behind a broad hall-pillar, far beyond
The sound of merriment and chorus bland:
He startled her; but soon she knew his face,
And grasp'd his fingers in her palsied hand,
Saying, 'Mercy, Porphyro! hie thee from this place;
They are all here to-night, the whole blood-thirsty race!

XII

'Get hence! get hence! there's dwarfish Hildebrand;
He had a fever late, and in the fit
He cursed thee and thine, both house and land:
Then there's that old Lord Maurice, not a whit
More tame for his gray hairs – Alas me! flit!
Flit like a ghost away.' – 'Ah, Gossip dear,

We're safe enough; here in this arm-chair sit,
And tell me how' – 'Good saints! not here, not here;
Follow me, child, or else these stones will be thy bier.'

XIII

He follow'd through a lowly arched way,
Brushing the cobwebs with his lofty plume,
And as she mutter'd 'Well-a – well-a-day!'
He found him in a little moonlight room,
Pale, lattic'd, chill, and silent as a tomb.
'Now tell me where is Madeline,' said he,
'O tell me, Angela, by the holy loom
Which none but secret sisterhood may see,
When they St. Agnes' wool are weaving piously.'

XIV

'St. Agnes! Ah! it is St. Agnes' Eve –
Yet men will murder upon holy days:
Thou must hold water in a witch's sieve,
And be liege-lord of all the Elves and Fays,
To venture so: it fills me with amaze
To see thee, Porphyro! – St. Agnes' Eve!
God's help! my lady fair the conjuror plays
This very night: good angels her deceive!
But let me laugh awhile, I've mickle time to grieve.'

XV

Feebly she laugheth in the languid moon,
While Porphyro upon her face doth look,
Like puzzled urchin on an aged crone
Who keepeth clos'd a wond'rous riddle-book,
As spectacled she sits in chimney nook.
But soon his eyes grew brilliant, when she told
His lady's purpose; and he scarce could brook
Tears, at the thought of those enchantments cold,
And Madeline asleep in lap of legends old.

XVI

Sudden a thought came like a full-blown rose,
Flushing his brow and in his pained heart
Made purple riot: then doth he propose
A stratagem, that makes the beldame start:
'A cruel man and impious thou art:
Sweet lady, let her pray, and sleep, and dream
Alone with her good augels, far apart
From wicked men like thee. Go, go! – I deem
Thou canst not surely be the same that thou didst seem.'

XVII

'I will not harm her, by all saints I swear,'
Quoth Porphyro: 'O may I ne'er find grace
When my weak voice shall whisper its last prayer,
If one of her soft ringlets I displace,
Or look with ruffian passion in her face:
Good Angela, believe me by these tears;
Or I will, even in a moment's space,
Awake, with horrid shout, my foemen's ears,
And beard them, though they be more fang'd than
wolves and bears.'

XVIII

'Ah! why wilt thou affright a feeble soul?
A poor, weak, palsy-stricken, churchyard thing,
Whose passing-bell may ere the midnight toll;
Whose prayers for thee, each morn and evening,
Were never miss'd.' – Thus plaining, doth she bring
A gentler speech from burning Porphyro;
So woful, and of such deep sorrowing,
That Angela gives promise she will do
Whatever he shall wish, betide her weal or woe.

XIX

Which was, to lead him, in close secrecy,
Even to Madeline's chamber, and there hide

Him in a closet, of such privacy
That he might see her beauty unespied,
And win perhaps that night a peerless bride,
While legion'd fairies pac'd the coverlet,
And pale enchantment held her sleepy-eyed.
Never on such a night have lovers met,
Since Merlin paid his Demon all the monstrous debt.

XX

'It shall be as thou wishest,' said the Dame:
'All cates and dainties shall be stored there
Quickly on this feast-night: by the tambour frame
Her own lute thou wilt see: no time to spare,
For I am slow and feeble, and scarce dare
On such a catering trust my dizzy head.
Wait here, my child, with patience; kneel in prayer
The while: Ah! thou must needs the lady wed,
Or may I never leave my grave among the dead.'

XXI

So saying, she hobbled off with busy fear.
The lover's endless minutes slowly pass'd;
The dame return'd, and whisper'd in his ear
To follow her; with aged eyes aghast
From fright of dim espial. Safe at last,
Through many a dusky gallery, they gain
The maiden's chamber, silken, hush'd, and chaste;
Where Porphyro took covert, pleas'd amain.
His poor guide hurried back with agues in her brain.

XXII

Her falt'ring hand upon the balustrade,
Old Angela was feeling for the stair,
When Madeline, St. Agnes' charmed maid,
Rose, like a mission'd spirit, unaware:
With silver taper's light, and pious care,
She turn'd, and down the aged gossip led

To a safe level matting. Now prepare,
   Young Porphyro, for gazing on that bed;
She comes, she comes again, like ring-dove fray'd and
fled.

XXIII

   Out went the taper as she hurried in;
   Its little smoke, in pallid moonshine, died:
   She clos'd the door, she panted, all akin
   To spirits of the air, and visions wide:
   No uttered syllable, or, woe betide!
   But to her heart, her heart was voluble,
   Paining with eloquence her balmy side;
   As though a tongueless nightingale should swell
Her throat in vain, and die, heart-stifled, in her dell.

XXIV

   A casement high and triple-arch'd there was,
   All garlanded with carven imag'ries,
   Of fruits, and flowers, and bunches of knot-grass,
   And diamonded with panes of quaint device,
   Innumerable of stains and splendid dyes,
   As are the tiger-moth's deep-damask'd wings;
   And in the midst, 'mong thousand heraldries,
   And twilight saints, and dim emblazonings,
A shielded scutcheon blush'd with blood of queens and
kings.

XXV

   Full on this casement shone the wintry moon,
   And threw warm gules on Madeline's fair breast,
   As down she knelt for heaven's grace and boon;
   Rose-bloom fell on her hands, together prest,
   And on her silver cross soft amethyst,
   And on her hair a glory, like a saint:
   She seem'd a splendid angel, newly drest,
   Save wings, for heaven: – Porphyro grew faint:
She knelt, so pure a thing, so free from mortal taint.

XXVI

Anon his heart revives: her vespers done,
    Of all its wreathed pearls her hair she frees;
    Unclasps her warmed jewels one by one;
    Loosens her fragrant boddice; by degrees
    Her rich attire creeps rustling to her knees:
    Half-hidden, like a mermaid in sea-weed,
    Pensive awhile she dreams awake, and sees,
    In fancy, fair St. Agnes in her bed,
But dares not look behind, or all the charm is fled.

XXVII

Soon, trembling in her soft and chilly nest,
    In sort of wakeful swoon, perplex'd she lay,
    Until the poppied warmth of sleep oppress'd
    Her soothed limbs, and soul fatigued away;
    Flown, like a thought, until the morrow-day;
    Blissfully haven'd both from joy and pain;
    Clasp'd like a missal where swart Paynims pray;
    Blinded alike from sunshine and from rain,
As though a rose should shut, and be a bud again.

XXVIII

Stol'n to this paradise, and so entranced,
    Porphyro gazed upon her empty dress,
    And listen'd to her breathing, if it chanced
    To wake into a slumberous tenderness;
    Which when he heard, that minute did he bless,
    And breath'd himself: then from the closet crept,
    Noiseless as fear in a wide wilderness,
    And over the hush'd carpet, silent, stept,
And 'tween the curtains peep'd, where, lo! – how fast
she slept.

XXIX

Then by the bed-side, where the faded moon
    Made a dim, silver twilight, soft he set
    A table, arid, half anguish'd, threw thereon

A cloth of woven crimson, gold, and jet: –
O for some drowsy Morphean amulet!
The boisterous, midnight, festive clarion,
The kettle-drum, and far-heard clarionet,
Affray his ears, though but in dying tone: –
The hall door shuts again, and all the noise is gone.

XXX

And still she slept an azure-lidded sleep,
In blanched linen, smooth, and lavender'd,
While he from forth the closet brought a heap
Of candied apple, quince, and plum, and gourd;
With jellies soother than the creamy curd,
And lucent syrops, tinct with cinnamon;
Manna and dates, in argosy transferr'd
From Fez; and spiced dainties, every one,
From silken Samarcand to cedar'd Lebanon.

XXXI

These delicates he heap'd with glowing hand
On golden dishes and in baskets bright
Of wreathed silver: sumptuous they stand
In the retired quiet of the night,
Filling the chilly room with perfume light. –
'And now, my love, my seraph fair, awake!
Thou art my heaven, and I thine eremite:
Open thine eyes, for meek St. Agnes' sake,
Or I shall drowse beside thee, so my soul doth ache.'

XXXII

Thus whispering, his warm, unnerved arm
Sank in her pillow. Shaded was her dream
By the dusk curtains: – 'twas a midnight charm
Impossible to melt as iced stream:
The lustres salvers in the moonlight gleam;
Broad golden fringe upon the carpet lies:
It seem'd he never, never could redeem

From such a stedfast spell his lady's eyes;
So mus'd awhile, entoil'd in woofed phantasies.

XXXIII

Awakening up, he took her hollow lute, –
Tumultuous, – and, in chords that tenderest be,
He play'd an ancient ditty, long since mute,
In Provence call'd, 'La belle dame sans mercy':
Close to her ear touching the melody; –
Wherewith disturb'd, she utter'd a soft moan:
He ceased – she panted quick – and suddenly
Her blue arayed eyes wide open shone:
Upon his knees he sank, pale as smooth-sculptured stone.

XXXIV

Her eyes were open, but she still beheld,
Now wide awake, the vision of her sleep:
There was a painful change, that nigh expell'd
The blisses of her dream so pure and deep
At which fair Madeline began to weep,
And moan forth witless words with many a sigh;
While still her gaze on Porphyro would keep;
Who knelt, with joined hands and piteous eye,
Fearing to move or speak, she look'd so dreamingly.

XXXV

'Ah, Porphyro!' said she, 'but even now
Thy voice was at sweet tremble in mine ear,
Made tuneable with every sweetest vow;
And those sad eyes were spiritual and clear:
How chang'd thou art! how pallid, chill, and drear!
Give me that voice again, my Porphyro,
Those looks immortal, those complainings dear!
Oh leave me not in this eternal woe,
For if thou diest, my Love, I know not where to go.'

XXXVI

Beyond a mortal man impassion'd far
At these voluptuous accents, he arose,
Ethereal, flush'd, and like a throbbing star
Seen mid the sapphire heaven's deep repose;
Into her dream he melted, as the rose
Blendeth its odour with the violet, –
Solution sweet: meantime the frost-wind blows
Like Love's alarum pattering the sharp sleet
Against the window-panes; St. Agnes' moon hath set.

XXXVII

'Tis dark: quick pattereth the flaw-blown sleet:
'This is no dream, my bride, my Madeline!'
'Tis dark: the iced gusts still rave and beat:
'No dream, alas! alas! and woe is mine!
Porphyro will leave me here to fade and pine. –
Cruel! what traitor could thee hither bring?
I curse not, for my heart is lost in thine,
Though thou forsakest a deceived thing; –
A dove forlorn and lost with sick unpruned wing.'

XXXVIII

'My Madeline! sweet dreamer! lovely bride!
Say, may I be for aye thy vassal blest?
Thy beauty's shield, heart-shap'd and vermeil dyed?
Ah, silver shrine, here will I take my rest
After so many hours of toil and quest,
A famish'd pilgrim, – saved by miracle.
Though I have found, I will not rob thy nest
Saving of thy sweet self; if thou think'st well
To trust, fair Madeline to no rude infidel.

XXXIX

'Hark! 'tis an elfin-storm from faery land,
Of haggard seeming, but a boon indeed:
Arise – arise! the morning is at hand; –
The bloated wassaillers will never heed: –

Let us away, my love, with happy speed;
There are no ears to hear, or eyes to see, –
Drown'd all in Rhenish and the sleep mead:
Awake! arise! my love, and fearless be,
For o'er the southern moors I have a home for thee.'

XL

She hurried at his words, beset with fears,
For there were sleeping dragons all around,
At glaring watch, perhaps, with ready spears –
Down the wide stairs a darkling way they found. –
In all the house was heard no human sound.
A chain-droop'd lamp was flickering by each door;
The arras, rich with horseman, hawk, and hound,
Flutter'd in the besieging wind's uproar;
And the long carpets rose along the gusty floor.

XLI

They glide, like phantoms, into the wide hall;
Like phantoms, to the iron porch, they glide;
Where lay the Porter, in uneasy sprawl,
With a huge empty flaggon by his side:
The wakeful bloodhound rose, and shook his hide,
But his sagacious eye an inmate owns:
By one, and one, the bolts full easy slide: –
The chains lie silent on the footworn stones; –
The key turns, and the door upon its hinges groans.

XLII

And they are gone: ay, ages long ago
These lovers fled away into the storm.
That night the Baron dreamt of many a woe,
And all his warrior-guests, with shade and form
Of witch, and demon, and large coffin-worm,
Were long be-nightmar'd. Angela the old
Died palsy-twitch'd, with meagre face deform;
The Beadsman, after thousand aves told,
For aye unsought for slept among his ashes cold.

'Ode on Indolence'

'They toil not, neither do they spin.'

I

One morn before me were three figures seen,
    With bowed necks, and joined hands, side-faced;
And one behind the other stepp'd serene,
    In placid sandals, and in white robes graced;
        They pass'd, like figures on a marble urn,
    When shifted round to see the other side;
They came again; as when the urn once more
        Is shifted round, the first seen shades return;
    And they were strange to me, as may betide
With vases, to one deep in Phidian lore.

II

How is it, Shadows! that I knew ye not?
    How came ye muffled in so hush a mask?
Was it a silent deep-disguised plot
    To steal away, and leave without a task
        My idle days? Ripe was the drowsy hour;
    The blissful cloud of summer-indolence
Benumb'd my eyes; my pulse grew less and less;
        Pain had no sting, and pleasure's wreath no flower:
    O, why did ye not melt, and leave my sense
Unhaunted quite of all but – nothingness?

III

A third time pass'd they by, and, passing, turn'd
    Each one the face a moment whiles to me;
Then faded, and to follow them I burn'd
    And ached for wings, because I knew the three;
        The first was a fair Maid, and Love her name;
    The second was Ambition, pale of cheek,
And ever watchful with fatigued eye;
        The last, whom I love more, the more of blame
    Is heap'd upon her, maiden most unmeek, –
I knew to be my demon Poesy.

IV

They faded, and, forsooth! I wanted wings:
　　O folly! What is Love? and where is it?
And for that poor Ambition! it springs
　　From a man's little heart's short fever-fit;
　　　　For Poesy! – no, – she has not a joy, –
　　At least for me, – so sweet as drowsy noons,
And evenings steep'd in honied indolence;
　　　　O, for an age so shelter'd from annoy,
　　That I may never know how change the moons,
Or hear the voice of busy common-sense!

V

And once more came they by, – alas! wherefore?
　　My sleep had been embroider'd with dim dreams;
My soul had been a lawn besprinkled o'er
　　With flowers, and stirring shades, and baffled beams:
　　　　The morn was clouded, but no shower fell,
　　Tho' in her lids hung the sweet tears of May;
The open casement press'd a new-leaved vine,
　　　　Let in the budding warmth and throstle's lay;
　　O Shadows! 'twas a time to bid farewell!
Upon your skirts had fallen no tears of mine.

VI

So, ye three Ghosts, adieu! Ye cannot raise
　　My head cool-bedded in the flowery grass;
For I would not be dieted with praise,
　　A pet-lamb in a sentimental farce!
　　　　Fade softly from my eyes, and be once more
　　In masque-like figures on the dreamy urn;
Farewell! I yet have visions for the night,
　　　　And for the day faint visions there is store;
　　Vanish, ye Phantoms! from my idle spright,
Into the clouds, and never more return!

Part III

ARRIVAL

From *The Bostonians* (1886)
by Henry James
(1843–1916)

The novel was criticized for attacking, as readers thought, the feminist culture of Boston, from which Verena Tarrant is whirled away by the masterful young southerner, Basil Ransome. The ending suggests that the reader himself must decide whether it is better to lead a safe life with bossy women, or accept the dangers of the dominant masculine world.

Olive was close at hand, on the threshold of the room, and as soon as Ransom looked at her he became aware that the weakness she had just shown had passed away. She had straightened herself again, and she was upright in her desolation. The expression of her face was a thing to remain with him for ever; it was impossible to imagine a more vivid presentment of blighted hope and wounded pride. Dry, desperate, rigid, she yet wavered and seemed uncertain; her pale, glittering eyes straining forward, as if they were looking for death. Ransom had a vision, even at that crowded moment, that if she could have met it there and then, bristling with steel or lurid with fire, she would have rushed on it without a tremor, like the heroine that she was. All this while the great agitation in the hall rose and fell, in waves and surges, as if Selah Tarrant and the agent were talking to the multitude, trying to calm them, succeeding for the moment, and then letting them loose again. Whirled down by one of the fitful gusts, a lady and a gentleman issued from the passage, and Ransom, glancing at them, recognized Mrs Farrinder and her husband.

'Well, Miss Chancellor,' said that more successful woman, with considerable asperity, 'if this is the way you're going to reinstate our sex!' She passed rapidly through the room, followed by Amariah, who remarked in his transit that it seemed as if there had been a want of organization, and the two retreated expeditiously, without the lady's having taken the smallest notice of Verena, whose conflict with her mother prolonged itself. Ransom, striving, with all needful consideration for Mrs Tarrant, to separate these two, addressed not a word to Olive; it was the last of her, for him, and he neither saw how her livid face suddenly glowed, as if Mrs Farrinder's words had been a lash, nor how, as if with a sudden inspiration, she rushed to the approach to the platform. If he had observed her, it might have seemed to him that she hoped to find the fierce expiation she sought for in exposure to the thousands she had disappointed and deceived, in offering herself to be trampled to death and torn to pieces. She might have suggested to him some feminine firebrand of Paris revolutions, erect on a barricade, or even the sacrificial figure of Hypatia, whirled through the furious mob of Alexandria. She was arrested an instant by the arrival of Mrs Burrage and her son, who had quitted the stage on observing the withdrawal of the Farrinders, and who swept into the room in the manner of people seeking shelter from a thunderstorm. The mother's face expressed the well-bred surprise of a person who should have been asked out to dinner and seen the cloth pulled off the table; the young man, who supported her on his arm, instantly lost himself in the spectacle of Verena disengaging herself from Mrs Tarrant, only to be again overwhelmed, and in the unexpected presence of the Mississippian. His handsome blue eyes turned from one to the other, and he looked infinitely annoyed and bewildered. It even seemed to occur to him that he might, perhaps, interpose with effect, and he evidently would have liked to say that, without really bragging, he would at least have kept the affair from turning into a row. But Verena, muffled and escaping, was deaf to him, and Ransom didn't look the right person to address such a remark as that to. Mrs Burrage and Olive, as the latter shot past, exchanged a glance which represented quick irony on one side and indiscriminating defiance on the other.

'Oh, are *you* going to speak?' the lady from New York inquired, with her cursory laugh.

Olive had already disappeared; but Ransom heard her

answer flung behind her into the room. 'I am going to be hissed and hooted and insulted!'

'Olive, Olive!' Verena suddenly shrieked; and her piercing cry might have reached the front. But Ransom had already, by muscular force, wrenched her away, and was hurrying her out, leaving Mrs Tarrant to heave herself into the arms of Mrs Burrage, who, he was sure, would, within the minute, loom upon her attractively through her tears, and supply her with a reminiscence, destined to be valuable, of aristocratic support and clever composure. In the outer labyrinth hasty groups, a little scared, were leaving the hall, giving up the game. Ransom, as he went, thrust the hood of Verena's long cloak over her head, to conceal her face and her identity. It quite prevented recognition, and as they mingled in the issuing crowd he perceived the quick, complete, tremendous silence which, in the hall, had greeted Olive Chancellor's rush to the front. Every sound instantly dropped, the hush was respectful, the great public waited, and whatever she should say to them (and he thought she might indeed be rather embarrassed), it was not apparent that they were likely to hurl the benches at her. Ransom, palpitating with his victory, felt now a little sorry for her, and was relieved to know that, even when exasperated, a Boston audience is not ungenerous. 'Ah, now I am glad!' said Verena, when they reached the street. But though she was glad, he presently discovered that, beneath her hood, she was in tears. It is to be feared that with the union, so far from brilliant, into which she was about to enter, these were not the last she was destined to shed.

'Kubla Khan'
by Samuel Taylor Coleridge
(1772–1834)

This, the most famous of Coleridge's poems, is a tender fantasy as full of freakish gaiety as of the odd workings of Coleridge's inner mind. He considered Kubla Khan a freak himself, making the notorious claim that if 'a person from Porlock' hadn't interrupted him while he was writing down the words heard or composed during an opium dream, the poem might have shaped itself into an extended masterpiece instead of remaining as a fragment. Of course he knew quite well that this was not the case; but his own fantasy of his poem's composition becomes virtually part of the poem itself.

The damsel with the dulcimer is an endearingly unserious figure, a comfortable romantic figment whose song contrasts most strikingly with the sudden intensity of his poem's 'ending', in which the poet makes an almost and altogether earnest claim for his calling, yet puts it before his readers as if they were playing a children's game together.

The printed texts of the poems have 'twice five miles of fertile ground': Coleridge's own MS, however, reads 'six', which in its context sounds a more magical number than 'five'. Coleridge has also overlaid with romantic magic ('But oh! that deep romantic chasm which slanted/ Down the green hill athwart a cedarn cover!') the very real and wild West Country landscape on Exmoor where the poem was written.

> In Xanadu did Kubla Khan
>   A stately pleasure-dome decree:
> Where Alph, the sacred river, ran
> Through caverns measureless to man
>   Down to a sunless sea.
> So twice five miles of fertile ground
>   With walls and towers were girdled round:
> And there were gardens bright with sinuous rills
> Where blossomed many an incense-bearing tree;

And here were forests ancient as the hills,
Enfolding sunny spots of greenery.

But O, that deep romantic chasm which slanted
Down the green hill athwart a cedarn cover!
A savage place! as holy and enchanted
As e'er beneath a waning moon was haunted
By woman wailing for her demon-lover!
And from this chasm, with ceaseless turmoil seething,
As if this earth in fast thick pants were breathing,
A mighty fountain momently was forced;
Amid whose swift half-intermitted burst
Huge fragments vaulted like rebounding hail,
Or chaffy grain beneath the thresher's flail:
And 'mid these dancing rocks at once and ever
It flung up momently the sacred river.
Five miles meandering with a mazy motion
Through wood and dale the sacred river ran,
Then reached the caverns measureless to man,
And sank in tumult to a lifeless ocean:
And 'mid this tumult Kubla heard from far
Ancestral voices prophesying war!

    The shadow of the dome of pleasure
       Floated midway on the waves;
    Where was heard the mingled measure
       From the fountain and the caves.
  It was a miracle of rare device,
  A sunny pleasure-dome with caves of ice!

A damsel with a dulcimer
  In a vision once I saw:
It was an Abyssinian maid,
  And on her dulcimer she played,
Singing of Mount Abora.
Could I revive within me,
Her symphony and song,

To such a deep delight 'twould win me,
That with music loud and long,
I would build that dome in air,
That sunny dome! those caves of ice!
And all who heard should see them there,
And all should cry, Beware! Beware!
His flashing eyes, his floating hair!
Weave a circle round him thrice,
    And close your eyes with holy dread,
    For he on honey-dew hath fed,
And drunk the milk of Paradise.

'April 1885'
by Robert Bridges
(1844–1930)

Poet Laureate Robert Bridges is not much read today, although his long poem, 'The Testament of Beauty' (1928) was much admired until quite recently, and is still well worth digging into, although not much recommends itself as hand luggage. This short poem is another matter. The wonderful subtlety of its metre contrasts with the simplicity of its feeling for one fine morning in a spring which, like most other English springs, was mostly cold and wet.

Wanton with long delay the gay spring leaping cometh;
The blackthorn starreth now his bough on the eve of May:
All day in the sweet box-tree the bee for pleasure hummeth:
The cuckoo sends afloat his note on the air all day.

Now dewy nights again and rain in gentle shower
At root of tree and flower have quenched the winter's drouth:
On high the hot sun smiles, and banks of cloud uptower
In bulging heads that crowd for miles the dazzling south.

From *A Fairly Honourable Defeat* (1968)
by Iris Murdoch
(1919–99)

This passage is the most incisive comment I know on the drop-out culture of the time; and also, incidentally, on our right to keep our sex lives to ourselves. Young Peter has been trying to needle his mother and father, Rupert and Hilda, and their friends, the homosexual couple Axel and Simon. But Axel bites back.

'Why don't *you* tell the truth!' said Peter. He pointed a long arm at Axel, who stopped in his tracks.

'What do you mean?'

'You keep your relationship with Simon a dark secret, don't you! Oh you let *us* know because we're your so-called dear friends and we're discreet. You can rely on us to tell lies on your behalf. But you'd die if everyone knew. You'd be ashamed!'

'I would not be ashamed!' said Axel, in a voice electric with anger.

'Peter, please come inside, come with me!' cried Hilda.

'Why do you lie about it then? Why don't you tell everyone in Whitehall that you live with another man? Are you afraid of losing your precious job? Afraid of being called a pansy? Why don't you tell the truth to the world?'

'Peter, *stop that!*' cried Rupert. He tore himself away from the wall, opening his arms helplessly.

Axel was silent for a moment. Then he said in a cold voice, 'My private life is my own affair. And would be if I were heterosexual. Why should I tell Whitehall whom I sleep with? I don't reject this society. I live and work in it and make my own judgements about how this is best to be done. You accuse us of hypocrisy. All right. Very few human beings are innocent of that. But I think you should also consider your own case. Let me suggest this. Why do you refuse to continue your education? Not for the reasons which you so loudly profess. But because you are afraid to compete intellectually with your peers, you are afraid of measuring yourself against other people, you are afraid of turning out to be third rate. So you decide not to compete at all. You retire into your dream world of drugs and layabouts and fuzzy fragments of Eastern philosophy about which you really understand nothing, and you call that reality. If you want to change our society, and I agree it needs changing, you must first learn how to think, and that requires a kind of humility which you show no sign of possessing. You imagine you've stepped out of society. You haven't and you can't. You're nothing but a symptom of corruption, a miserable little scab upon the body politic. You're a part of the thing and you seem to prefer to be a powerless and unconscious part. If you really want to get out of it you'd better emigrate or commit suicide.'

There was a loud crash and a wail from Hilda. Peter had hurled his glass across the pool where it broke into fragments against the farther edge. Peter turned and disappeared through the drawing room doors, banging them behind him. Hilda struggled with the doors and followed him in. Morgan poured herself out another drink. She said, 'Well, well, well.'

Rupert walked round the pool and started picking up pieces of glass from the flagstones.

'I'm very sorry, Rupert,' said Axel.

'That's all right,' said Rupert. 'It was Peter's fault. I simply don't understand that boy.'

'Have a drink, Rupert,' said Morgan. 'You need one.'

'Thanks.'

'It wasn't Peter's fault,' said Axel. 'At least not entirely. And I ought not to have lost my temper. The fact is he said something that was true and it upset me extremely.'

'You don't mean – ?' said Morgan.

'I probably ought to tell everyone in Whitehall. Only I'm not going to. Simon, we're leaving. I do apologize, Rupert.'

Axel marched away and through the French windows. Simon said 'Oh dear, oh dear' and was about to follow him when Morgan said 'Wait'. She turned him round by the shoulders and very carefully took off the crown of roses and laid it down on the table. Then she kissed him lingeringly upon the cheek. 'Don't worry, Simon.' Simon said 'Darling!', fluttered his hands and ran after Axel. Rupert sat down.

'Cheer up, Rupert,' said Morgan. She touched his hair. 'Young people are terribly cruel.'

'The Falling of the Leaves'
by W. B. Yeats
(1865–1939)

Yeats' boast was that he was always remaking himself as a man and a poet: an impressive achievement both ways. His early poems have a charm which he shook off ruthlessly, and the later ones have a hardness which in its way is just as much the Yeatsian magic as the land of faery with which he began.

Autumn is over the long leaves that love us,
And over the mice in the barley sheaves;
Yellow the leaves of the rowan above us,
And yellow the wet wild-strawberry leaves.

The hour of the waning of love has beset us,
And weary and worn are our sad souls now;
Let us part, ere the season of passion forget us,
With a kiss and a tear on thy drooping brow.

'The Black Tower'

Say that the men of the old black tower
Though they but feed as the goatherd feeds,
Their money spent, their wine gone sour,
Lack nothing that a soldier needs,
That all are oath-bound men;
Those banners come not in.

There in the tomb stand the dead upright,
But winds come up from the shore;
They shake when the winds roar
Old bones upon the mountain shake.

Those banners come to bribe or threaten
Or whisper that a man's a fool
Who when his own right king's forgotten
Cares what king sets up his rule.
If he died long ago
Why do you dread us so?

There in the tomb drops the faint moonlight
But wind comes up from the shore.
They shake when the winds roar
Old bones upon the mountain shake.

The tower's old cook that must climb and clamber
Catching small birds in the dew of the morn
When we hale men lie stretched in slumber
Swears that he hears the great king's horn.
But he's a lying hound;
Stand we on guard oath-bound!

There in the tomb the dark grows blacker,
But wind comes up from the shore.
They shake when the winds roar
Old bones upon the mountain shake.

'The Second Coming'

Turning and turning in the widening gyre
The falcon cannot hear the falconer;
Things fall apart; the centre cannot hold;
Mere anarchy is loosed upon the world,
The blood-dimmed tide is loosed, and everywhere
The ceremony of innocence is drowned;
The best lack all conviction, while the worst
Are full of passionate intensity.

Surely some revelation is at hand;
Surely the Second Coming is at hand.
The Second Coming! Hardly are those words out
When a vast image out of *Spiritus Mundi*
Troubles my sight: somewhere in sands of the desert
A shape with lion body and the head of a man,
A gaze blank and pitiless as the sun,
Is moving its slow thighs, while all about it
Reel shadows of the indignant desert birds.
The darkness drops again; but now I know
That twenty centuries of stony sleep
Were vexed to nightmare by a rocking cradle,
And what rough beast, its hour come round at last,
Slouches towards Bethlehem to be born?

'Dis Aliter Visum; or, Le Byron se nos Jours'
by Robert Browning (1812–89)

I don't quite know why I am particularly fond of this poem of Browning's since I am fond of so many of his poems, and particularly those that are a kind of short story in verse.

The atmosphere of this one, and the magic of its interrelated 'streams of consciousness' shine with many meanings, and tell us much about the age and the social world in which they were written.

'Dis aliter visum' – seen otherwise by the Gods.

I
Stop, let me have the truth of that!
    Is that all true? I say, the day
Ten years ago when both of us
    Met on a morning, friends – as thus
We meet this evening, friends or what? –

II
Did you – because I took your arm
    And sillily smiled, 'A mass of brass
'That sea looks, blazing underneath!'
    While up the cliff-road edged with heath,
We took the turns nor came to harm –

III
Did you consider 'Now makes twice
    'That I have seen her, walked and talked
'With this poor pretty thoughtful thing,
    'Whose worth I weigh: she tries to sing;
'Draws, hopes in time the eye grows nice;

IV
'Reads verse and thinks she understands;
    'Loves all, at any rate, that's great,
'Good, beautiful; but much as we
    'Down at the bath-house love the sea,
'Who breathe its salt and bruise its sands:

V

'While . . . do but follow the fishing-gull
  'That flaps and floats from wave to cave!
'There's the sea-lover, fair my friend!
  'What then? Be patient, mark and mend!
'Had you the making of your scull?'

VI

And did you, when we faced the church
  With spire and sad slate roof, aloof
From human fellowship so far,
  Where a few graveyard crosses are,
And garlands for the swallows' perch, –

VII

Did you determine, as we stepped
  O'er the lone stone fence, 'Let me get
'Her for myself, and what's the earth
  'With all its art, verse, music, worth –
'Compared with love, found, gained, and kept?

VIII

'Schumann's our music-maker now;
  'Has his march-movement youth and mouth?
'Ingres's the modern man that paints;
  'Which will lean on me, of his saints?
'Heine for songs; for kisses, how?'

IX

And did you, when we entered, reached
  The votive frigate, soft aloft
Riding on air this hundred years,
  Safe-smiling at old hopes and fears, –
Did you draw profit while she preached?

X

Resolving, 'Fools we wise men grow!
   'Yes, I could easily blurt out curt
'Some question that might find reply
   'As prompt in her stopped lips, dropped eye,
'And rush of red to cheek and brow:

XI

'Thus were a match made, sure and fast,
   ''Mid the blue weed-flowers round the mound
'Where, issuing, we shall stand and stay
   'For one more look at baths and bay,
'Sands, sea-gulls, and the old church last –

XII

'A match 'twixt me, bent, wigged and lamed,
   'Famous, however, for verse and worse,
'Sure of the Fortieth spare Arm-chair
   'When gout and glory seat me there,
'So, one whose love-freaks pass unblamed, –

XIII

'And this young beauty, round and sound
   'As a mountain-apple, youth and truth
'With loves and doves, at all events
   'With money in the Three per Cents;
'Whose choice of me would seem profound: –

XIV

'She might take me as I take her.
   'Perfect the hour would pass, alas!
'Climb high, love high, what matter? Still,
   'Feet, feelings, must descend the hill:
'An hour's perfection can't recur.

XV

'Then follows Paris and full time
   'For both to reason: "Thus with us!"

'She'll sigh, "Thus girls give body and soul
 "'At first word, think they gain the goal,
"'When 't is the starting-place they climb!

XVI

"'My friend makes verse and gets renown;
 "'Have they all fifty years, his peers?
"'He knows the world, firm, quiet and gay;
 "'Boys will become as much one day:
'They're fools; he cheats, with beard less brown.

XVII

"'For boys say, *Love me or I die!*
 "'He did not say, *The truth is, youth*
"'*I want, who am old and know too much;*
 "'I'd catch youth: lend me sight and touch!
"'*Drop heart's blood where life's wheels grate dry!"*

XVIII

'While I should make rejoinder' – (then
 It was, no doubt, you ceased that least
Light pressure of my arm in yours)
 "'I can conceive of cheaper cures
"'For a yawning-fit o'er books and men.

XIX

"'What? All I am, was, and might be,
 "'All, books taught, art brought, life's whole strife,
"'Painful results since precious, just
 "'Were fitly exchanged, in wise disgust,
"'For two cheeks freshened by youth and sea?

XX

"'All for a nosegay! – what came first;
 "'With fields on flower, untried each side;
"'I rally, need my books and men,
 "'And find a nosegay": drop it, then,
'No match yet made for best or worst!'

XXI

That ended me. You judged the porch
   We left by, Norman; took our look
At sea and sky; wondered so few
   Find out the place for air and view;
Remarked the sun began to scorch;

XXII

Descended, soon regained the baths,
   And then, good-bye! Years ten since then:
Ten years! We meet: you tell me, now,
   By a window-seat for that cliff-brow,
On carpet-stripes for those sand-paths.

XXIII

Now I may speak: you fool, for all
   Your lore! WHO made things plain in vain?
What was the sea for? What, the grey
   Sad church, that solitary day,
Gosses and graves and swallows' call?

XXIV

Was there nought better than to enjoy?
   No feat which, done, would make time
And let us pent-up creatures through
   Into eternity, our due?
No forcing earth teach heaven's employ?

XXV

No wise beginning, here and now,
   What cannot grow complete (earth's feat)
And heaven must finish, there and then?
   No tasting earth's true food for men,
Its sweet in sad, its sad in sweet?

XXVI

No grasping at love, gaining a share
  O' the sole spark from God's life at strife
With death, so, sure of range above
  The limits here? For us and love,
Failure; but, when God fails, despair.

XXVII

This you call wisdom? Thus you add
  Good unto good again, in vain?
You loved, with body worn and weak;
  I loved, with faculties to seek:
Were both loves worthless since ill-clad?

XXVIII

Let the mere star-fish in his vault
  Crawl in a wash of weed, indeed,
Rose-jacynth to the finger-tips:
  He, whole in body and soul, outstrips
Man, found with either in default.

XXIX

But what's whole, can increase no more,
  Is dwarfed and dies, since here's its sphere.
The devil laughed at you in his sleeve!
  You knew not? That I well believe;
Or you had saved two souls: nay, four.

XXX

For Stephanie sprained last night her wrist,
  Ankle or something. 'Pooh,' cry you?
At any rate she danced, all say,
  Vilely; her vogue has had its day.
Here comes my husband from his whist.

The Big Sleep (1939)
by Raymond Chandler (1888–1959)

The final page. No need for me to explain what is going on: Chandler's rich but never mannered prose does it all for one. The Big Sleep *is a classic of fiction, not just of the detective story.*

'He'll try to kill you.'

'Yeah,' I said. 'His best boy couldn't. I'll take a chance on the others. Does Norris know?'

'He'll never tell.'

'I thought he knew.'

I went quickly away from her down the room and out and down the tiled staircase to the front hall. I didn't see anybody when I left. I found my hat alone this time. Outside the bright gardens had a haunted look, as though small wild eyes were watching me from behind the bushes, as though the sunshine itself had a mysterious something in its light. I got into my car and drove off down the hill.

What did it matter where you lay once you were dead? In a dirty sump or in a marble tower on top of a high hill. You were dead, you were sleeping the big sleep, you were not bothered by things like that. Oil and water were the same as wind and air to you. You just slept the big sleep, not caring about the nastiness of how you died or where you fell. Me, I was part of the nastiness now. Far more a part of it than Rusty Regan was. But the old man didn't have to be. He could lie quiet in his canopied bed, with his bloodless hands folded on the sheet, waiting. His heart was a brief, uncertain murmur. His thoughts were as grey as ashes. And in a little while he too, like Rusty Regan, would be sleeping the big sleep.

On the way downtown I stopped at a bar and had a couple of double Scotches. They didn't do me any good. All they did was make me think of Silver-Wig, and I never saw her again.

From *Good Bones*

by Margaret Atwood

(1939–)

Margaret Atwood puts her finger on what is really succulent and sumptuous in Raymond Chandler's world, his passion for furniture and the appearance of those tacky Los Angeles rooms where something nasty has occurred.

An affair with Raymond Chandler, what a joy! Not because of the mangled bodies and the marinated cops and hints of eccentric sex, but because of his interest in furniture. He knew that furniture could breathe, could feel, not as we do but in a way more muffled, like the word *upholstery*, with its overtones of mustiness and dust, its bouquet of sunlight on ageing cloth or of scuffed leather on the backs and seats of sleazy office chairs. I think of his sofas, stuffed to roundness, satin-covered, pale-blue like the eyes of his cold blonde unbodied murderous women, beating very slowly, like the hearts of hibernating crocodiles; of his chaises longues, with their malicious pillows. He knew about front lawns too, and greenhouses, and the interiors of cars.

This is how our love affair would go. We would meet at a hotel, or a motel, whether expensive or cheap it wouldn't matter. We would enter the room, lock the door, and begin to explore the furniture, fingering the curtains, running our hands along the spurious gilt frames of the pictures, over the real marble or the chipped enamel of the luxurious or tacky washroom sink, inhaling the odour of the carpets, old cigarette smoke and spilled gin and fast meaningless sex or else the rich abstract scent of the oval transparent soaps imported from England, it wouldn't matter to us; what would matter would be our response to the furniture, and the furniture's response to us. Only after we had sniffed, fingered, rubbed, rolled on and absorbed the furniture of the room would we fall into each other's arms, and onto the bed (king-sized? peach-coloured? creaky? narrow? four-posted? pioneer-quilted? lime-green chenille-covered?), ready at last to do the same things to each other.

From *Journals* 1990–92

by Anthony Powell

(1905–2000)

Anthony Powell was getting on himself when Graham Greene died, but one understands his surprise. Greene somehow seemed an institution that was there for ever. These passages from his later Journals *show what a good critic he was, always mixing his own brand of local knowledge with darts of uninhibited perception.*

Wednesday, 3 April 1991

Graham Greene obit. This was rather a surprise. Thought Graham would live for ever like Somerset Maugham, even though I knew he had been in Switzerland (Vevey) unwell for several months. From the word go I had found his books wholly unreadable, long before there could have been any question of jealousy, fears of the imputation of which always prevented me from adversely criticizing them in print later. The plays I found are even worse. He was good at reportage, a lively journalist, able businessman, but the novels are vulgarized Conrad, to which tedious Roman Catholic propaganda is added, the occasional efforts at humour dreadful. In thinking this I am confronted by overwhelming popular taste for Greene not only by the public, but almost every writer of eminence, here or abroad. It seems to me Greene will settle like, say, Henry Seton Merriman, a novelist by no means without gifts (though he pinched a good deal from Turgenev in *The Sowers*, V always asserting that Conrad pinched from Merriman). It is of course true that a writer can reach a stage of general approbation when literary editors do not like a reviewer to attack him, reviewers themselves feeling it would be too much of a business to attempt to undermine a well-known name within a thousand words or so, much easier to accept in this case the world view.

There was always an element of deviousness, indeed

humbug, about all Graham's public utterances and behaviour. I think he was completely cynical, really only liking sex and money and his own particular form of publicity. I always got on pretty well with him, chiefly just before the war. We had the only colossal row after the war when he was my publisher. He would go white with rage on such occasions, admitting that he had to have rows from time to time for his health. One supposes he was extraordinarily good at assessing people, tho' in my opinion quite incapable of describing individuals with conviction.

He could be good company. I remember especially an evening I spent with him and Malcolm Muggeridge, when Graham described how he had sent a french letter stuffed with hundreds-and-thousands to Wilson Harris, a prim, pompous editor of the *Spectator*, whom Graham greatly disliked and richly deserved to be ragged. During the war I met Graham one evening tearing in a great hurry through St James's Square. He said: 'I've just discovered the Americans in my office [presumably MI6] don't do fire-watching. I'm going to put a stop to that.' It was quite late in the evening. The incident was typical of Graham's whole demeanour, delight in polemics, causing trouble.

The telephone was going all the morning, afternoon, from papers, media, asking for appreciations. I answered these by saying Graham and I were always on good terms, I used to write to him when he received a new decoration, etc., but we neither of us liked the other's books. I took this to be Graham's feeling, as he never mentioned mine, and once reviewing Evelyn Waugh he spoke of him coming under my influence 'with all the Ivos and Ivors'. All the same Graham's death rather unsettling for some reason.

Mr Moss called. Told him to do his usual £100 sort of maintenance on the drive. He said: 'Lovely to see you again.' Much relieved to find I can read Shakespeare in bed again, something I found myself too exhausted to do hitherto after turning in, since my indispositions. I was surprised how much I missed this, tho' it may sound affected.

Reread Z. Najda's (Polish) biography of Joseph Conrad, the only life of Conrad that is any good, being extremely good, though I emerge from the book with a less romantic view of Conrad than hitherto held. He was a very tricky character indeed. One sees why Henry James thought Conrad so 'rum'. He was punctilious about many things, but telling the truth was not one of them, while at least part of his 'rumness' seems to have been inability to come to terms with his own identity. On the one hand, anyway in early days, he took the line that he was not a professional writer, might easily go back to the sea, even take up some other job. Later, on the other hand, he used to be irritated by critics always mentioning his nautical past, referring to him as a writer about the sea.

True, many of Conrad's books are not about the sea, but he himself had always plugged that 'image'. At the same time he showed the greatest integrity as an artist from the start, only falling off a bit when hard up (which he was perpetually, however much he earned) towards the end of his career. His abilities and failings are of great interest. He was not at all scrupulous about borrowing money, Najda pointing out that Conrad always lived in the traditional manner of a Polish gentleman (about ten per cent of the country regarding itself as such, cf. Wales, where an even higher percentage did), regarding a certain amount of dash, debt, as a necessity. His friends thought Jessie awful, no doubt with reason, but the marriage obviously worked well. One would be interested to know who took Conrad (at a fairly mature age) to the Forty-Three (as reported in her Memoirs by its proprietress Mrs Meyrick), a London night-club of notable squalor.

Correspondence
by A. E. Housman
(1859–1936)

Housman was on excellent terms with his step-mother Lucy, and they often corresponded. This was his response to her offer to send him an anthology of devotional poetry.

I shall be interested to see the Devotional Poems. Perhaps I myself may write a Hymn-book for use in the Salvation Army:

> There is Hallelujah Hannah
>   Walking backwards down the lane,
> And I hear the loud Hosanna
>   Of regenerated Jane;
> And Lieutenant Isabella
>   In the centre of them comes,
> Dealing blows with her umbrella
>   On the trumpets and the drums.

Or again:

> 'Hallelujah!' was the only observation
> That escaped Lieutenant-Colonel Mary Jane,
> When she tumbled off the platform in the station,
> And was cut in little pieces by the train.
>   Mary Jane, the train is through yer:
>   Hallelujah, Hallelujah!
> We will gather up the fragments that remain.

It seems to come quite easy.

'Christmas at Sea'
by Robert Louis Stevenson
(1850–94)

I find 'Christmas at Sea' a very moving poem, much more so than most of Stevenson's work which tends to be brilliantly written but rather unfeeling (Henry James thought so too.) Some of his poetry is also rather sentimental, but certainly not this poem. And as befits a man whose father and grandfather were lighthouse builders, Stevenson is as interested as Kipling was in technical matters. His ship, probably a full-rigged ship (like the Cutty Sark*) sailing from a Scottish port, finds itself embayed by the gale between two headlands. The only way out is to set more sail: a dangerous procedure with swift shipwreck if the sails blow out, but a slower but sure one if the crew are cautious. Hence the mate's warning, and the captain's answer. 'It's the one way or the other, Mr Jackson, he replied.'*

The sheets were frozen hard, and they cut the naked hand;
The decks were like a slide, where a seaman scarce could
    stand,
The wind was a nor'-wester, blowing squally off the sea;
And cliffs and spouting breakers were the only things a-lee.

They heard the surf a-roaring before the break of day;
But 'twas only with the peep of light we saw how ill we lay.
We tumbled every hand on deck instanter, with a shout,
And we gave her the maintops'l, and stood by to go about.

All day we tack'd and tack'd between the South Head and the
    North;
All day we haul'd the frozen sheets, and got no further forth;
All day as cold as charity, in bitter pain and dread,
For very life and nature we tack'd from head to head.

We gave the South a wider berth, for there the tide-race
      roar'd;
But every tack we made we brought the North Head close
      aboard;
So's we saw the cliffs and houses, and the breakers running
      high,
And the coastguard in his garden, with his glass against his eye.

The frost was on the village roofs as white as ocean foam;
The good red fires were burning bright in every 'longshore
      home;
The windows sparkled clear, and the chimneys volley'd out;
And I vow we sniff'd the victuals as the vessel went about.

The bells upon the church were rung with a mighty jovial
      cheer;
For it's just that I should tell you how (of all days in the year)
This day of our adversity was blessèd Christmas morn,
And the house above the coastguard's was the house where I
      was born.

O well I saw the pleasant room, the pleasant faces there,
My mother's silver spectacles, my father's silver hair;
And well I saw the firelight, like a flight of homely elves
Go dancing round the china-plates that stand upon the shelves!

And well I knew the talk they had, the talk that was of me,
Of the shadow on the household and the son that went to sea;
And O the wicked fool I seem'd, in every kind of way,
To be here and hauling frozen ropes on blessed Christmas
      Day.

They lit the high sea-light, and the dark began to fall.
'All hands to loose topgallant sails!' I heard the captain call.
'By the Lord, she'll never stand it,' our first mate Jackson
      cried.
. . . 'It's the one way or the other, Mr. Jackson,' he replied.

She stagger'd to her bearings, but the sails were new and good,
And the ship smelt up to windward just as though she under-
    stood.
As the winter's day was ending, in the entry of the night,
We clear'd the weary headland, and pass'd below the light.

And they heaved a mighty breath, every soul on board but
    me,
As they saw her nose again pointing handsome out to sea;
But all that I could think of, in the darkness and the cold,
Was just that I was leaving home and my folks were growing
    old.

From *The House in Paris* (1935)
by Elizabeth Bowen
(1899–1973)

I've commented already on the marvellous seductiveness of Elizabeth Bowen when you first encounter her, her strange, infinitely vivid prose, whether describing a winter's morning in Regent's Park, or going by ship up the River Lee to Cork.

On the left shore, a steeple pricked up out of a knoll of trees, above a snuggle of gothic villas; then there was the sad stare of what looked like an orphanage. A holy bell rang and a girl at a corner mounted her bicycle and rode out of sight. The river kept washing salt off the ship's prow. Then, to the right, the tree-dark hill of Tivoli began to go up, steep, with pallid stucco houses appearing to balance on the tops of trees. Palladian columns, gazebos, glass-houses, terraces showed on the background misted with spring green, at the tops of shafts or on toppling brackets of rock, all stuck to the hill, all slipping past the ship . . .

The river still narrowing, townish terraces of tall pink houses under a cliff drew in. In one fanlight stood a white plaster horse; clothes were spread out to dry on a briar bush. Someone watching the ship twitched back a curtain; a woman leaned out signalling with a mirror: several travellers must be expected home. A car with handkerchiefs fluttering drove alongside the ship. On the city side, a tree-planted promenade gave place to boxy warehouses; a smoky built-over hill appeared beyond Tivoli. But Cork consumes its own sound: the haze remained quite silent.

The Death of the Heart (1938)

That morning's ice, no more than a brittle film, had cracked and was now floating in segments. These tapped together or, parting, left channels of dark water, down which swans in slow indignation swam. The islands stood in frozen woody brown dusk: it was now between three and four in the afternoon. A sort of breath from the clay, from the city outside the park, condensing, made the air unclear; through this, the trees round the lake soared frigidly up. Bronze cold of January bound the sky and the landscape; the sky was shut to the sun – but the swans, the rims of the ice, the pallid withdrawn Regency terraces had an unnatural burnish, as though cold were light. There is something momentous about the height of winter. Steps rang on the bridges, and along the black walks. This weather had set in; it would freeze harder tonight.

On a footbridge between an island and the mainland a man and woman stood talking, leaning on the rail. In the intense cold, which made everyone hurry, they had chosen to make this long summerlike pause. Their oblivious stillness made them look like lovers – actually, their elbows were some inches apart; they were riveted not to each other but to what she said. Their thick coats made their figures sexless and stiff as chessmen: they were well-to-do, inside bulwarks of fur and cloth their bodies generated a steady warmth; they could only see the cold – or, if they felt it, they only felt it at their extremities. Now and then he stamped on the bridge, or she brought her muff up to her face. Ice pushed down the channel under the bridge, so that while they talked their reflections were constantly broken up.

He said: 'You were mad ever to touch the thing.'

'All the same, I feel sure you would have, St Quentin.'

'No, I doubt that. I never do want to know, really, what anyone thinks.'

'If I'd had the slightest idea –'

'However, you did.'

'And I've seldom been more upset.'

'Poor Anna! . . . How did you find it, though?'

'Oh, I wasn't looking for it,' said Anna quickly. 'I should far rather not know that the thing existed, and till then, you see, I'd had no idea that it did. Her white dress came back with one of mine from the cleaners; I unpacked mine because I wanted to put it on, then, as Matchett was out that day, I took hers up to hang it up in her room. Portia was out at lessons, of course. Her room looked, as I've learnt to expect, shocking: she has all sorts of arrangements Matchett will never touch. You know what some servants are – how they ride one down, and at the same time make all sorts of allowance for temperament in children or animals.'

'You would call her a child?'

'In ways, she's more like an animal. I made that room so pretty before she came. I had no idea how blindly she was going to live. Now I hardly ever go in there; it's simply discouraging.'

St Quention said rather vaguely: 'How annoying for you!' He had screwed round his head inside the folds of his scarf, to consider Anna with abstract attentiveness. For she had this little way of travestying herself and her self-pities, till the view she took of herself, when she was with him, seemed to concert exactly with the view he took of her sex. She wrote herself down like this, obligingly, to suit him, with a touch of friendly insolence. He saw in this over-acting a kind of bluffing, which made him like Anna, whom he liked much more. Her smoothness of contour, her placid derisive smile, her way of drawing her chin in when she did smile, often made him think of a sardonic bland white duck. But there seemed no doubt at this moment that, beyond acting, she was really put out: her chin was tucked inside her big fur collar, and under the fur cap she wore peaked forward her forehead was wrinkled up. She was looking down unhappily at her muff, with her fine blonde lashes cast on her cheek; now and then a hand came out of her muff and she dabbed at the tip of her nose with a handkerchief. She could feel St Quentin looking, but took no notice: she detected the touch of malice in his pity for women.

'All I did,' she went on, 'when I had hung her dress up, was to take one look round, rather feeling I ought. As usual, my heart sank; I really did feel it was time I took a line. But she and I are on such curious terms – when I ever do take a line, she never knows what it is. She is so unnaturally callous about *objects* – she treats any hat, for instance, like an old envelope. Nothing that's hers ever seems, if you know what I mean, to belong to her: which makes it meaningless to give her any present, unless it's something to eat, and she doesn't always like that. It may be because they always lived in hotels. Well, one thing I had thought she'd like was a little *escritoire* thing that came from Thomas's mother's – her father may well have used it. I'd had that put in her room. It has drawers that lock and quite a big flap to write on. The flap locks too: I hoped that would make her see that I quite meant her to have a life of her own. You know, though it may seem rash, we even give her a latchkey. But she seems to have lost the keys – nothing was locked, and there was no sign of them.'

'How annoying!' said St Quentin again.

'It was indeed. Because if only – However . . . Well, that wretched little *escritoire* caught my eye. She had crammed it, but really, stuffed it, as though it were a bin. She seems to like hoarding paper; she gets almost no letters, but she'd been keeping all sorts of things Thomas and I throw away – begging letters, for instance, or quack talks about health. As Matchett would say, it gave me rather a turn.'

'When you opened the desk?'

'Well, it looked so awful, you see. The flap would not shut – papers gushed out all round it and even stuck through the hinge. Which made me shake with anger – I really can't tell you why. So I scooped the papers all out and dropped them into the armchair – I intended to leave them there, then tell her she must be tidy. Under the papers were some exercise books with notes she had taken at her lessons, and under the exercise books this diary, which, as I say, I read. One of those wretched black books one buys for about a shilling with *moiré* outsides . . . After that, of course I had to put everything back the way it was.'

'Exactly as it had been?'

'Exactly, I'm quite certain. One may never reproduce the same muddle exactly, but she would never know.'

There was a pause, and St Quentin looked at a seagull. Then he said: 'How inconvenient it all is!'

Inside her muff, Anna drove her hands together; raising her eyes she looked angrily down the lake. 'She's made nothing but trouble since before she was born.'

'You mean, it's a pity she ever was?'

'Well, naturally, I feel that at the moment. Though I would rather, of course, that you didn't say so – she is Thomas's sister after all.'

'But don't you think perhaps you exaggerate? The agitation of seeing something quite unexpected often makes one think it worse than it is.'

'That diary could not be worse than it is. That is to say, it couldn't be worse for me. At the time, it only made me superficially angry – but I've had time since then to think it over in. And I haven't quite finished yet – I keep remembering more things.'

'Was it very . . . unkind?'

'No, not meant to be that. No, she'd like to help us, I'm sure.

'Then, mawkish, you mean?'

'I mean, more, completely distorted and distorting. As I read I thought, either this girl or I are mad. And I don't think I am, do you?'

'Surely not. But why should you be so upset if it simply shows what is the matter with her? Was it affected?'

'Deeply hysterical.'

'You've got to allow for style, though. Nothing arrives on paper as it started, and so much arrives that never started at all. To write is always to rave a little – even if one did once know what one meant, which at her age seems unlikely. There are ways and ways of trumping a thing up: one gets more discriminating not necessarily more honest. *I* should know, after all.'

'I am sure you do, St Quentin. But this was not a bit like your beautiful books. In fact it was not like *writing* at all.'

She paused and added: 'She was so odd about me.'

St Quentin, looking frustrated, started feeling about for his handkerchief. He blew his nose and went on, with iron determination: 'Style is the thing that's always a bit phony, and at the same time you cannot write without style. Look how much goes to addressing an envelope – for, after all, it's a matter of set-out. And a diary, after all, is written to please oneself – therefore it's bound to be enormously written up. The obligation to write it is all in one's own eye, and look how one is when it's almost always written – upstairs, late, overwrought, alone . . . All the same, Anna, it must have interested you.'

'It opened at my name.'

'So you read straight on from there?'

'No, it opened at the last entry; I read that, then went back and started from the beginning. The latest entry was about dinner the evening before.'

'Let's see: had you a party?'

'No, no: much worse than that. It had been simply her and me and Thomas. She must have bolted upstairs and written everything down. Naturally, when I'd read that I went back to the beginning, to see what had got her into that state of mind. I still don't see why she wrote the thing at all.'

'Perhaps', said St Quentin mildly, 'she's interested in experience for its own sake.'

'How could she be, yet? At her age, look how little she's got. Experience isn't interesting till it begins to repeat itself – in fact, till it does that, it hardly *is* experience.'

'Tell me, do you remember the first sentence of all?'

'Indeed I do,' Anna said. '"*So I am with them, in London*".'

'With a comma after the "them"? . . . The comma is good; that's style . . . I should like to have seen it, I must say.'

'Still, I'm glad you didn't, St Quentin. It might make you not come to our house again. Or, if you did still come, it might make you not talk.'

From 'The Rubaiyat of Omar Khayyam'
by Edward FitzGerald
(1809–83)

As poetry, FitzGerald's poem is virtually his own, as he knew little or nothing of the language of Omar Khayyam, who in Persia was not considered the equal of great poets like Firdausi. Omar Khayyam was an epigrammatist concerned, as a fellow-poet of his time put it, 'to stick a fingernail into your heart'.

Robert Graves and his Farsi speaker have put the poem into literal English, which shows how blunt and pointed its native effects were. FitzGerald changed the tone completely, and in his successive revisions (not all of which are by any means an improvement) he made the poem elegiac, mournfully ironic and traditionally English, decorated with his oriental names and situations.

Some of the verses that he fiddled about with and discarded retain a charming and, what seem at times an almost accidental, felicity, like his plea to his friends to lay him 'shrouded in the living leaf/By some not unfrequented garden-side'.

A book of Verses underneath the Bough,
A Jug of Wine, a Loaf of Bread – and Thou
   Beside me singing in the Wilderness –
O, Wilderness were Paradise enow!

Some for the Glories of This World; and some
Sigh for the Prophet's Paradise to come;
   Ah, take the Cash, and let the Credit go,
Nor heed the rumble of a distant Drum!

Look to the blowing Rose about us – 'Lo,
Laughing,' she says, 'into the world I blow.
   At once the silken tassel of my Purse
Tear, and its Treasure on the Garden throw.'

And those who husbanded the Golden grain
And those who flung it to the winds like Rain,
    Alike to no such aureate Earth are turned
As, buried once, Men want dug up again.

The Worldly Hope men set their Hearts upon
Turns Ashes – or it prospers; and anon,
    Like Snow upon the Desert's dusty Face,
Lighting a little hour or two – is gone.

Think, in this battered Caravanserai
Whose Portals are alternate Night and Day,
    How Sultan after Sultan with his Pomp
Abode his destined Hour, and went his way.

They say the Lion and the Lizard keep
The Courts where Jamshyd gloried and drank deep:
    And Bahram, that great Hunter – the wild Ass
Stamps o'er his Head, but cannot break his Sleep.

I sometimes think that never blows so red
The Rose as where some buried Caesar bled;
    That every Hyacinth the Garden wears
Dropt in her Lap from some once lovely Head.

And this reviving Herb whose tender Green
Fledges the River-Lip on which we lean –
    Ah, lean upon it lightly! or who knows
From what once lovely Lip it springs unseen!

Ah, my Beloved, fill the Cup that clears
TO-DAY of past Regrets and future Fears:
    To-morrow! – Why, To-morrow I may be
Myself with Yesterday's Seven thousand Years.

For some we loved, the loveliest and the best
That from his Vintage rolling Time hath prest,

Have drunk their Cup a Round or two before,
And one by one crept silently to rest.

And we, that now make merry in the Room
They left, and Summer dresses in new bloom,
  Ourselves must we beneath the Couch of Earth
Descend – ourselves to make a Couch – for whom?

Ah, make the most of what we yet may spend,
Before we too into the Dust descend;
  Dust into Dust, and under Dust to lie,
Sans Wine, sans Song, sans Singer, and – sans End!

From *The Return of the Native* (1878)
by Thomas Hardy
(1840–1928)

There is no need to explain why a passage like this stays in the mind. Hardy's Egdon – 'the great heath' – is more a country of the mind than a real place, just because it has been taken over so completely as a part of the atmosphere of Hardy's novels.

A Saturday afternoon in November was approaching the time of twilight, and the vast tract of unenclosed wild known as Egdon Heath embrowned itself moment by moment. Overhead the hollow stretch of whitish cloud shutting out the sky was as a tent which had the whole heath for its floor.

The heaven being spread with this pallid screen and the earth with the darkest vegetation, their meeting-line at the horizon was clearly marked. In such contrast the heath wore the appearance of an instalment of night which had taken up its place before its astronomical hour was come: darkness had to a great extent arrived hereon, while day stood distinct in the sky. Looking upwards, a furze-cutter would have been inclined to continue work; looking down, he would have decided to finish his faggot and go home. The distant rims of the world and of the firmament seemed to be a division in time no less than a division in matter. The face of the heath by its mere complexion added half an hour to evening, it could in like manner retard the dawn, sadden noon, anticipate the frowning of storms scarcely generated, and intensify the opacity of a moonless midnight to a cause of shaking and dread.

In fact, precisely at this transitional point of its nightly roll into darkness the great and particular glory of the Egdon waste began, and nobody could be said to understand the heath who had not been there at such a time. It could best be felt when it could not clearly be seen, its complete effect and explanation lying in this and the succeeding hours before the next dawn:

then, and only then, did it tell its true tale. The spot was, indeed, a near relation of night, and when night showed itself an apparent tendency to gravitate together could be perceived in its shades and the scene. The sombre stretch of rounds and hollows seemed to rise and meet the evening gloom in pure sympathy, the heath exhaling darkness as rapidly as the heavens precipitated it. And so the obscurity in the air and the obscurity in the land closed together in a black fraternization towards which each advanced half-way.

The place became full of a watchful intentness now; for when other things sank brooding to sleep the heath appeared slowly to awake and listen. Every night its Titanic form seemed to await something; but it had waited thus, unmoved, during so many centuries, through the crises of so many things, that it could only be imagined to await one last crisis – the final over-throw.

It was a spot which returned upon the memory of those who loved it with an aspect of peculiar and kindly congruity. Smiling champaigns of flowers and fruit hardly do this, for they are permanently harmonious only with an existence of better reputation as to its issues than the present. Twilight combined with the scenery of Egdon Heath to evolve a thing majestic without severity, impressive without showiness, emphatic in its admonitions, grand in its simplicity. The qualifications which frequently invest the façade of a prison with far more dignity than is found in the façade of a palace double its size lent to this heath a sublimity in which spots renowned for beauty of the accepted kind are utterly wanting. Fair prospects wed happily with fair times; but alas, if times be not fair! Men have oftener suffered from the mockery of a place too smiling for their reason than from the oppression of surroundings oversadly tinged. Haggard Egdon appealed to a subtler and scarcer instinct, to a more recently learnt emotion, than that which responds to the sort of beauty called charming and fair.

Indeed, it is a question if the exclusive reign of this orthodox beauty is not approaching its last quarter. The new Vale of Tempe may be a gaunt waste of Thule: human souls may find themselves in closer and closer harmony with external things wearing a sombreness distasteful to our race when it was young. The time seems near, if it has not actually arrived, when the chastened sublimity of a moor, a sea, or a mountain will be all of nature that is absolutely in keeping with the moods of the more thinking among mankind. And ultimately, to the commonest tourist, spots like Iceland may become what the vineyards and myrtle-gardens of South Europe are to him now; and Heidelberg and Baden be passed unheeded as he hastens from the Alps to the sand-dunes of Scheveningen.

The most thorough-going ascetic could feel that he had a natural right to wander on Egdon: he was keeping within the line of legitimate indulgence when he laid himself open to influences such as these. Colours and beauties so far subdued were, at least, the birthright of all. Only in summer days of highest feather did its mood touch the level of gaiety. Intensity was more usually reached by way of the solemn than by way of the brilliant, and such a sort of intensity was often arrived at during winter darkness, tempests, and mists. Then Egdon was aroused to reciprocity; for the storm was its lover, and the wind its friend. Then it became the home of strange phantoms; and it was found to be the hitherto unrecognized original of those wild regions of obscurity which are vaguely felt to be compassing us about in midnight dreams of flight and disaster, and are never thought of after the dream till revived by scenes like this.

It was at present a place perfectly accordant with man's nature – neither ghastly, hateful, nor ugly: neither commonplace, unmeaning, nor tame; but, like man, slighted and enduring; and withal singularly colossal and mysterious in its swarthy monotony. As with some persons who have long lived apart, solitude seemed to look out of its countenance. It had a lonely face, suggesting tragical possibilities. This obscure, obsolete, superseded country figures in Domesday. Its condition is recorded therein as that of heathy, furzy, briary wilderness – 'Bruaria'. Then follows the length and breadth in leagues; and, though some uncertainty exists as to the exact extent of this ancient lineal measure, it appears from the figures that the area of Egdon down to the present day has but little diminished. 'Turbaria Bruaria' – the right of cutting heath-turf – occurs in charters relating to the district. 'Overgrown with heth and mosse,' says Leland of the same dark sweep of country.

Here at least were intelligible facts regarding landscape – far-reaching proofs productive of genuine satisfaction. The untameable, Ishmaelitish thing that Egdon now was it always had been. Civilization was its enemy; and ever since the beginning of vegetation its soil had worn the same antique brown dress, the natural and invariable garment of the particular formation. In its venerable one coat lay a certain vein of satire on human vanity in clothes. A person on a heath in raiment of modern cut and colours has more or less an anomalous look. We seem to want the oldest and simplest human clothing where the clothing of the earth is so primitive.

To recline on a stump of thorn in the central valley of Egdon between afternoon and night, as now, where the eye could reach nothing of the world outside the summits and shoulders of heathland which filled the whole circumference of its glance, and to know that everything around and underneath had been from prehistoric times as unaltered as the stars overhead, gave ballast to the mind adrift on change, and harassed by the irrepressible New. The great inviolate place had an ancient permanence which the sea cannot claim. Who can say of a particular sea that it is old? Distilled by the sun, kneaded by the moon, it is renewed in a year, in a day, or in an hour. The sea changed, the fields changed, the rivers, the villages and the people changed, yet Egdon remained. Those surfaces were neither so steep as to be destructible by weather, nor so flat as to be the victims of floods and deposits. With the exception of an aged highway, and a still more aged barrow presently to be referred to – themselves almost crystallized to natural products by long continuance - even the trifling irregularities were not caused by pickaxe, plough, or spade, but remained as the very finger-touches of the last geological change.

The above-mentioned highway traversed the lower levels of

the heath, from one horizon to another. In many portions of its course it overlaid an old vicinal way, which branched from the great Western road of the Romans, the Via Iceniana, or Ikenild Street, hard by. On the evening under consideration it would have been noticed that, though the gloom had increased sufficiently to confuse the minor features of the heath, the white surface of the road remained almost as clear as ever.

'A Trophy of Arms'
by Ruth Pitter
(1897–1992)

Ruth Pitter, who had a very long life, in the course of which she improbably became a friend of the young George Orwell, was almost blind at one point, but continued indomitably writing poems. Not many are good, but the ones that are, such as, 'A Trophy of Arms', are very good indeed.

The primrose awakens, but
I lean here alone
Where the proud helmet is cut
In the hard stone:
Where the true sword is hung
With the straight spear,
When all is said and sung
My heart is here.

A nameless tomb I guard,
I know not for whose sake,
Nor for what far reward;
Yet I hear wake
The voice of honour, calling
From the bones I have cherished:
'The mighty are not fallen,
Nor the weapons of war perished.'

'A Song'
by George Darley
(1795–1846)

'A Song' is an imitation – and a brilliant one – of a Caroline lyric. Appearing anonymously, it took in the scholars of the time, but today it seems very much of a piece with the mermaid song which follows, and with Darley's own touching and highly personal flavour as a poet. Aldous Huxley remarked in his superior way, 'those seals are absurd but they make the poem'. They do indeed. And they make it very touching. Their sealy life somehow conveys all those simple connubial joys which the poor mermaids know nothing about. At least Darley evidently thought they didn't. He was a rather melancholy bachelor, and perhaps he was thinking of himself.

It is not Beauty I demand,
    A crystal brow, the moon's despair
Nor the snow's daughter, a white hand,
    Nor mermaid's yellow pride of hair.

Tell me not of your starry eyes,
    Your lips that seem on roses fed,
Your breasts where Cupid tumbling lies,
    Nor sleeps for kissing of his bed.

A bloomy pair of vermeil cheeks,
    Like Hebe's in her ruddiest hours,
A breath that softer music speaks
    Than summer winds a-wooing flowers.

These are but gauds; nay, what are lips?
    Coral beneath the ocean-stream,
Whose brink when your adventurer [s]ips
    Full oft he perisheth on them.

And what are cheeks but ensigns oft
    That wave hot youth to fields of blood?
Did Helen's breast, though ne'er so soft,
    Do Greece or Ilium any good?

Eyes can with baleful ardour burn,
    Poison can breath that erst perfumed,
There's many a white hand holds an urn
    With lovers' hearts to dust consumed.

For crystal brows, there's naught within,
    They are but empty cells for pride;
He who the syren's hair would win
    Is mostly strangled in the tide.

Give me, instead of beauty's bust,
    A tender heart, a loyal mind,
Which with temptation I could trust,
    Yet never linked with error find.

One in whose gentle bosom, I
    Could pour my secret heart of woes,
Like the care-burthened honey-fly
    That hides his murmurs in the rose.

My earthly comforter! whose love
    So indefeasible might be,
That when my spirit won above
    Hers could not stay for sympathy.

'The Mermaiden's Vesper Hymn'

Troop home to silent grots and caves!
   Troop home, and mimic as you go
The mournful winding of the waves,
   Which to their dark abysses flow!

At this sweet hour all things beside
   In amorous pairs to covert creep:
The swans that brush the evening tide,
   Homeward in snowy couples keep.

In his green den the murmuring seal
   Close by his sleek companion lies;
While singly we to bedward steal,
   And close in fruitless sleep our eyes.

In bowers of love men take their rest,
   In loveless bowers we sigh alone, –
With bosom-friends are others blest,
   But we have none! but we have none!

'Hoopoe'

D. H. Lawrence might have made us see the Hoopoe more closely, but Darley somehow evokes it without description.

Solitary wayfarer!
Minstrel winged of the green wild!
What dost thou delaying here,
Like a wood-bewildered child
Weeping to his far-flown troop,
Whoop! and plaintive whoop! and whoop!
Now from rock and now from tree,
Bird! methinks thou whoop'st to me,
Flitting before me upward still
With clear warble, as I've heard
Oft on my native Northern hill
No less wild and lone a bird,
Luring me with his sweet chee-chee
Up the mountain crags which he
Tript as lightly as a bee,

O'er steep pastures, far among
Thickets, and briary lanes along,
Following still a fleeting song! –
If such my errant nature, I
Vainly to curb or coop it try,
Now that the sundrop thro' my frame,
Kindles another soul of flame!
Whoop on, whoop on, thou canst not wing
Too fast or far, thou well-named thing,
Hoopoe, if of that tribe which sing
Articulate in the desert ring!

'Felix Randal'

by Gerard Manley Hopkins (1844–89)

One of Hopkins' most moving and memorable poems, also one of the easist to read, understand and remember. Hopkins as the priest in a northern parish uses, very simply and effectively, northern speech ('Being anointed and all . . . all road ever he offended'). He was in charge, for some time, of the souls in a parish which would have contained a blacksmith, perhaps a sick one like Felix Randal.

Felix Randal the farrier, O is he dead then? my duty all ended,
Who have watched his mould of man, big-boned and hardy-
    handsome
Pining, pining, till time when reason rambled in it and some
Fatal four disorders, fleshed there, all contended?

Sickness broke him. Impatient, he cursed at first, but mended
Being anointed and all; though a heavenlier heart began some
Months earlier, since I had our sweet reprieve and ransom
Tendered to him. Ah well, God rest him all road ever he
    offended!

This seeing the sick endears them to us, us too it endears.
My tongue had taught thee comfort, touch had quenched thy
    tears,
Thy tears that touched my heart, child, Felix, poor Felix
    Randal;

How far from then forethought of, all thy more boisterous
    years,
When thou at the random grim forge, powerful amidst peers,
Didst fettle for the great grey drayhorse his bright and batter-
    ing sandal!

From 'A Year of Birds' (1933)
by Iris Murdoch (1919–99)

*Iris Murdoch sometimes wrote poetry and produced 'A Year of Birds'
which was set to music by Malcolm Williamson and sung during the
1993 Proms. The book was illustrated by her friend Reynolds Stone,
a wonderful artist and engraver.*

*Iris was fond of birds, though without knowing much about them. Both
of us were thrilled to see the storks in Spain who nest on house tops.*

'December'

When the dark hawberries hang down and drip like blood
And the old man's beard has climbed up high in the wood
And the golden bracken has been broken by the snows
And Jesus Christ has come again to heal and pardon,
Then the little robin follows me through the garden,
In the dark days his breast is like a rose.

'John Sees a Stork at Zamorra'

Walking among quiet people out from mass
He saw a sudden stork
Fly, from its nest upon a house.
So blue the sky, the bird so white,
For all these people an accustomed sight.
He took his hat off in sheer surprise
And stood and threw his arms out wide
Letting the people pass
Him by on either side
Aware of nothing but the stork-arise.

On a black tapestry now
This gesture of joy
So absolutely you.

'When We Two Parted'
by Lord Byron
(1788–1824)

*Byron is and was famous for all sorts of things, but his capacity to write
a perfect verse about parting and loss can still come to us with a shock of
surprise.*

When we two parted
  In silence and tears,
Half broken-hearted
  To sever for years,
Pale grew thy cheek and cold,
  Colder thy kiss;
Truly that hour foretold
  Sorrow to this.

The dew of the morning
  Sunk chill on my brow –
It felt like the warning
  Of what I feel now.
Thy vows are all broken,
  And light is thy fame;
I hear thy name spoken,
  And share in its shame.

They name thee before me,
  A knell to mine ear;
A shudder comes o'er me –
  Why wert thou so dear?
They know not I knew thee,
  Who knew thee too well: –
Long, long shall I rue thee,
  Too deeply to tell.

In secret we met —
In silence I grieve,
That thy heart could forget,
Thy spirit deceive.
If I should meet thee
After long years,
How should I greet thee?
With silence and tears.

'How Sleep the Brave'
by William Collins
(1721–59)

Patriotic mourning is a tricky subject for a poet to handle. After the event it can sound banal or embarrassing or both. The Ancient Greek model ('Stranger, go tell the Spartans that we lie here in obedience to their orders') is admirably terse and precise, but lacking in what we have come to think of as human feeling.

For a combination of restraint, good taste, and quiet emotional accuracy it would be difficult to beat our own eighteenth century, exemplified in this little masterpiece by Collins.

How sleep the brave, who sink to rest
By all their country's wishes blest!
When Spring, with dewy fingers cold,
Returns to deck their hallowed mould,
She there shall dress a sweeter sod
Than Fancy's feet have ever trod.

By fairy hands their knell is rung,
By forms unseen their dirge is sung;
There Honour comes, a pilgrim grey,
To bless the turf that wraps their clay,
And Freedom shall awhile repair
To dwell a weeping hermit there!

'The Burial of Sir John Moore at Corunna'
by Charles Wolfe
(1791–1823)

The personification of Honour and Freedom by Collins has a classic naturalness about it. They are the ideals for which men have died, or at least can justly be thought to have died. 'Fairy' was an adjective much less coy then than it is today; but since altering words in favourite poems is one of the pleasures of carrying them around in one's head, I usually amend the line in my mental memory. 'By forms unknown' would deftly balance 'by forms unseen' in the following line? And yet of course the poem, and its author, knew best. No created poem is perfect, but the cat of creation gives it the involuntary rightness of its own whole and separate personality.

From the English point of view the Seven Years War in Collins' time was in fact a ruthless and profitable struggle, the foundation of imperial power and glory in the century to follow.

In the first war of that century – the nineteenth – British troops were mostly engaged in Spain and casualties were a good deal heavier than they had been in eighteeth-century wars. One of them was Sir John Moore, a brilliant soldier who, if he had lived, might have commanded in the Peninsula War instead of his junior general, soon to become the Duke of Wellington.

Not a drum was heard, not a funeral note,
    As his corse to the rampart we hurried;
Not a soldier discharged his farewell shot
    O'er the grave where our hero we buried.

We buried him darkly at dead of night,
    The sods with our bayonets turning,
By the struggling moonbeam's misty light
    And the lanthorn dimly burning.

No useless coffin enclosed his breast,
    Not in sheet or in shroud we wound him;
But he lay like a warrior taking his rest
    With his martial cloak around him.

Few and short were the prayers we said,
    And we spoke not a word of sorrow;
But we steadfastly gazed on the face that was dead,
    And we bitterly thought of the morrow.

We thought, as we hollowed his narrow bed
    And smoothed down his lonely pillow,
That the foe and the stranger would tread o'er his head,
    And we far away on the billow!

Lightly they'll talk of the spirit that's gone,
    And o'er his cold ashes upbraid him –
But little he'll reck, if they let him sleep on
    In the grave where a Briton has laid him.

But half of our heavy task was done
    When the clock struck the hour for retiring;
And we heard the distant and random gun
    That the foe was sullenly firing.

Slowly and sadly we laid him down,
    From the field of his fame fresh and gory;
We carved not a line, and we raised not a stone,
    But we left him alone with his glory.

'Ode'

by Henry Timrod

(1828–67)

Charles Wolfe was, like Collins, a country parson, a peacetime parson who was never near a battlefield. But he read an account of Moore's burial some years after the event, and was moved to write the one poem for which he is remembered. He imagines himself as one of the common soldiers who buried Moore, and he does it very movingly, even though he assumes a bayonet could be used as a spade, not apparently realizing that it would be like digging a grave with an outsize knitting needle. Soldiers in fact carried picks and shovels as a matter of course.

And yet the poem shows that Wolfe possessed in full measure the Romantic imagination, and the Romantic poets' sense of memorable event.

This makes it all the more remarkable that the South Carolina poet Henry Timrod, writing 100 years after Collins, in the wake of the great American Civil War, should touch the reader's heart today by having composed a funeral ode for the Confederate dead, not in the flamboyant style of the Victorian age but in the quietly decorous and graceful manner of the previous century.

Sung on the occasion of decorating the graves of the Confederate dead, at Magnolia Cemetery, Charleston, S.C., 1867.

I

Sleep sweetly in your humble graves,
   Sleep, martyrs of a fallen cause;
Though yet no marble column craves
   The pilgrim here to pause.

II

In seeds of laurel in the earth
   The blossom of your fame is blown,
And somewhere, waiting for its birth,
   The shaft is in the stone!

III

Meanwhile, behalf the tardy years
   Which keep in trust your storied tombs,
Behold! your sisters bring their tears,
   And these memorial blooms.

IV

Small tributes! but your shades will smile
   More proudly on these wreaths to-day,
Than when some cannon-moulded pile
   Shall overlook this bay.

V

Stoop, angels, hither from the skies!
   There is no holier spot of ground
Than where defeated valor lies,
   By mourning beauty crowned!

'On a Vulgar Error'
by C. S. Lewis (1898–1963)

C. S. Lewis was a great Oxford character whose most memorable book was The Allegory of Love *(1936). He also wrote verses at times, in addition to his famous children's books, and these are two examples.*

As might be inferred from 'On a Vulgar Error', he was a man who, like George Orwell, 'loved the past, hated the present, and dreaded the future'.

No. It's an impudent falsehood. Men did not
Invariably think the newer way
Prosaic, mad, inelegant, or what not.

Was the first pointed arch esteemed a blot
Upon the church? Did anybody say
How modern and how ugly? They did not.

Plate-armour, or windows glazed, or verse fire-hot
With rhymes from France, or spices from Cathay,
Were these at first a horror? They were not.

If, then, our present arts, laws, houses, food
All set us hankering after yesterday,
Need this be only an archaising mood?

Why, any man whose purse has been let blood
By sharpers, when he finds all drained away
Must compare how he stands with how he stood.

If a quack doctor's breezy ineptitude
Has cost me a leg, must I forget straightway
All that I can't do now, all that I could?

So, when our guides unanimously decry
The backward glance, I think we can guess why.

'Ballade of Dead Gentlemen'

This piece shows Lewis in a game mood which came equally naturally to him. One can have fun discovering who the deceased are or what did, or may, have happened to them.

Where, in what bubbly land, below
    What rosy horizon dwells to-day
That worthy man Monsieur Cliquot
    Whose widow has made the world so gay?
    Where now is Mr Tanqueray?
Where might the King of Sheba be
    (Whose wife stopped dreadfully long away)?
Mais où sont messieurs les maris?

Say where did Mr Beeton go
    With rubicund nose and whiskers grey
To dream of dumplings long ago,
    Of syllabubs, soups, and *entremets*?
    In what dim isle did Twankey lay
His aching head? What murmuring sea
    Lulls him after the life-long fray?
Mais où sont messieurs les maris?

How Mr Grundy's cheeks may glow
    By a bathing-pool where lovelies play,
I guess, but shall I ever know?
    Where – if it comes to that, *who*, pray –
Is Mr Masham? Sévigné
    And Mr Siddons and Zebedee
And Gamp and Hemans, where are they?
Mais où sont messieurs les maris?

Princesses all, beneath your sway
    In this grave world they bowed the knee;
Libertine airs in Elysium say
    Mais où sont messieurs les maris?

'Mourning'
by Andrew Marvell
(1621–78)

Marvell is the most mysterious of poets, for no one seems to know what he was like or what he thought about life. In 'Mourning' he follows the metaphysical pattern of ingenuity, producing as many far-flung reasons as he can for the phenomenon of tears, and then suddenly in the eighth verse the whole tone of the poem changes and becomes indeed mysterious. Tears are not to be interpreted, nor grief understood.

The 'Horatian Ode' is a splendid and economical commentary on power, the execution of Charles I and the meteoric rise of Cromwell. Marvell, who with Milton was Secretary to the Commonwealth, and officially a Republican, could see the point of both sides. There was no party-line or political correctness for cultivated people in those days. We can't be sure what Marvell himself thought, any more than we know Shakespeare's views on politics – or if he had any.

I
You, that decipher out the fate
   Of human offsprings from the skies,
What mean these infants which, of late,
   Spring from the stars of Chlora's eyes?

II
Her eyes confused, and doubled o'er
   With tears suspended ere they flow,
Seem bending upwards to restore
   To Heaven, whence it came, their woe.

III
When, moulding of the watery spheres,
   Slow drops untie themselves away,
As if she with those precious tears
   Would strew the ground where Strephon lay.

IV

Yet some affirm, pretending art,
   Her eyes have so her bosom drowned,
Only to soften, near her heart,
   A place to fix another wound.

V

And, while vain pomp does her restrain
   Within her solitary bower,
She courts herself in amorous rain,
   Herself both Danae and the shower.

VI

Nay others, bolder, hence esteem
   Joy now so much her master grown,
That whatsoever does but seem
   Like grief is from her windows thrown.

VII

Nor that she pays, while she survives,
   To her dead love this tribute due,
But casts abroad these donatives,
   At the installing of a new.

VIII

How wide they dream! the Indian slaves,
   That sink for pearl through seas profound,
Would find her tears yet deeper waves,
   And not of one the bottom sound.

IX

I yet my silent judgment keep,
   Disputing not what they believe:
But sure as oft as women weep,
   It is to be supposed they grieve.

'An Horation Ode Upon Cromwell's Return from Ireland, 1650'

The forward youth that would appear
Must now forsake his Muses dear,
   Nor in the shadows sing
   His numbers languishing.

'Tis time to leave the books in dust,
And oil the unusèd armour's rust,
   Removing from the wall
   The corslet of the hall.

So restless Cromwell could not cease
In the inglorious arts of peace,
   But through adventurous war
   Urgèd his active star:

And like the three-forked lightning, first
Breaking the clouds where it was nurst,
   Did thorough his own side
   His fiery way divide:

For 'tis all one to courage high,
The emulous, or enemy;
   And with such, to enclose
   Is more than to oppose.

Then burning through the air he went
And palaces and temples rent;
   And Caesar's head at last
   Did through his laurels blast.

'Tis madness to resist or blame
The force of angry Heaven's flame;
   And if we would speak true,
   Much to the man is due,

Who, from his private gardens, where
He lived reservèd and austere
   (As if his highest plot
   To plant the bergamot),

Could by industrious valour climb
To ruin the great work of time,
   And cast the Kingdom old
   Into another mould.

Though Justice against Fate complain,
And plead the ancient rights in vain –
   But those do hold or break
   As men are strong or weak –

Nature, that hateth emptiness,
Allows of penetration less,
   And therefore must make room
   Where greater spirits come.

What field of all the civil wars
Where his were not the deepest scars?
   And Hampton shows what part
   He had of wiser art;

Where, twining subtle fears with hope,
He wove a net of such a scope
   That Charles himself might chase
   To Car'sbrook's narrow case;

That thence the Royal Actor borne
The tragic scaffold might adorn:
   While round the armèd bands
   Did clap their bloody hands.

He nothing common did or mean
Upon that memorable scene,
 But with his keener eye
 The axe's edge did try;

Nor called the Gods, with vulgar spite,
To vindicate his helpless right;
 But bowed his comely head
 Down, as upon a bed.

This was that memorable hour
Which first assured the forcèd power:
 So when they did design
 The Capitol's first line,

A bleeding head, where they begun,
Did fright the architects to run;
 And yet in that the State
 Foresaw its happy fate!

And now the Irish are ashamed
To see themselves in one year tamed:
 So much one man can do
 That does both act and know.

They can affirm his praises best,
And have, though overcome, confest
 How good he is, how just
 And fit for highest trust;

Nor yet grown stiffer with command,
But still in the Republic's hand –
 How fit he is to sway
 That can so well obey!

He to the Commons' feet presents
A Kingdom for his first year's rents,
    And, what he may, forbears
    His fame, to make it theirs:

And has his sword and spoils ungirt
To lay them at the public's skirt.
    So when the falcon high
    Falls heavy from the sky,

She, having killed, no more does search
But on the next green bough to perch,
    Where, when he first does lure,
    The falconer has her sure.

What may not then our Isle presume
While victory his crest does plume?
    What may not others fear,
    If thus he crown each year?

A Caesar he, ere long, to Gaul,
To Italy an Hannibal,
    And to all States not free
    Shall climacteric be.

The Pict no shelter now shall find
Within his particoloured mind,
    But from this valour sad
    Shrink underneath the plaid,

Happy, if in the tufted brake
The English hunter him mistake,
    Nor lay his hounds in near
    The Caledonian deer.

But thou, the War's and Fortune's son,
March indefatigably on;
    And for the last effect,
    Still keep thy sword erect:

Besides the force it has to fright
The spirits of the shady night,
    The same arts that did gain
    A power, must it maintain.

From *The Book of Kings*

11 And he said, Go forth, and stand upon the mount before the LORD. And, behold, the LORD passed by, and a great and strong wind rent the mountains, and brake in pieces the rocks before the Lord: *but* the LORD *was* not in the wind; and after the wind an earthquake; *but* the LORD *was* not in the earthquake:

12 And after the earthquake a fire: *but* the LORD *was* not in the fire; and after the fire a still small voice.

13 And it was so, when Elijah heard *it*, that he wrapped his face in his mantle, and went out, and stood in the entering in of the cave. And, behold, *there came* a voice unto him, and said, What doest thou here, Elijah?

Acknowledgements

The Literary Trustees of Walter de la Mare and The Society of Authors as their representative for 'The Round' and 'The Children of Stare'.

Curtis Brown for Elizabeth Bowen, *The Death of the Heart*.

The C. S. Lewis Company for poems by C. S. Lewis.

The Harvill Press for Anna Akhmatova, 'Lot's Wife'.

David Higham Associates for Anthony Powell, extract from *Journals*.

Enitharmon Press for Ruth Pitter, 'A Trophy of Arms'.

Jonathan Clowes Ltd, London, on behalf of the Literary Estate of Sir Kingsley Amis, for 'Nothing to Fear'.

John Murray (Publishers) Ltd for John Betjeman, 'How to Get On in Society' and 'Love in a Valley' from *Collected Poems*.

A. P. Watt on behalf of Michael B. Yeats for W. B. Yeats, 'Falling of Leaves'.

Faber and Faber for T. S. Eliot, 'La Figlia Che Piange'.

Faber and Faber for Philip Larkin, 'The Whitsun Weddings' and 'Marriages'.

Faber and Faber for W. H Auden, 'Musée des Beaux Arts'.

Faber and Faber for Marianne Moore, 'Marriage'.

Every effort has been made to locate holders of copyright material; however, the author and publishers would be interested to hear from any copyright holders not here acknowledged so that full acknowledgement may be made in future editions.

Index of Authors